WHERE
CAN I TURN FOR
PEACE?

WHERE CAN I TURN FOR PEACE?

JACK R. CHRISTIANSON, WAYNE BRICKEY, C. MAX CALDWELL, TONI SORENSON,
LEAUN G. OTTEN, E. DOUGLAS CLARK, TODD B. PARKER, JOY SAUNDERS LUNDBERG

Covenant Communications, Inc.

Cover image Prince of Peace © 2009 Liz Lemon Swindle. Used with permission from Foundation Arts. For print information, go to www.foundationarts.com or call 1-800-366-2781

Cover design copyrighted 2009 by Covenant Communications, Inc.

Published by Covenant Communications, Inc.
American Fork, Utah

Printed in Canada
First Printing: October 2009

16 15 14 13 12 11 10   10 9 8 7 6 5 4 3 2

ISBN-13 978-1-59811-863-6
ISBN-10 1-59811-863-3

TABLE OF CONTENTS

$\mathscr{J}$NTRODUCTION

———— ⚬⚬⚬ ————

We are living in very difficult times—times of economic uncertainty, global unrest, political upheaval. Drug abuse is rampant. Families are being shattered. Immorality has become the norm. Those in power are calling into question the values we hold dear.

Many have lost jobs. Some have lost fortunes. Too many have lost loved ones—those who have let go of their tenuous grip on the iron rod and who are wandering, lost, through the mists of darkness. Others have lost dreams. Some have lost hope. And a few have even lost faith.

No one, it seems, is immune.

We may feel as though we have lost our anchor. Our mooring is gone. We are adrift in a sea that is often turbulent. The water is so cold it chills our bones. The waves are unpredictable and not infrequently frightening. We are exhausted from frenetically paddling our arms and legs in an effort to stay afloat—but we have to keep paddling, no matter how exhausted we are.

We feel cut loose. Treacherously bobbing around in a great sea, surrounded by impossibly deep water, we yearn to find an anchor—a great, solid anchor that will tether us to safety and provide us stability. Most difficult of all, we may feel isolated in that vast sea. For what may be the first time in our lives, we may feel profoundly alone. We may feel small—almost indistinguishable in the vast, dark sea—and frightened.

We yearn for comfort. We cry out for peace.

That comfort is within our reach. That peace beckons.

It is available to us in our most trying and difficult circumstances. It is there to ease our battered hearts and souls. It is there because One has gone to the very depths, into vast reaches that we cannot even imagine. And He is there, waiting to encircle us with His renewing comfort and peace.

"Peace I leave with you," He assures, "my peace I give unto you: not as the world giveth, give I unto you" (John 14:27). That promise is sure, because the Promise-giver never wavers. We can count on Him who also tells us, "Let not your heart be troubled, neither let it be afraid" (John 14:27).

Jesus Christ, the Savior of all mankind, is uniquely qualified to make that promise—to offer us the peace and comfort we so desperately seek. Through some infinite arithmetic we cannot comprehend with our finite minds, He entered a peaceful hillside garden two millennia ago and took upon Himself our suffering. As He writhed in agony beneath the olive trees, He took upon Himself not only our sins, but all other things we could possibly suffer—our sicknesses, our pains, our emotional grief, our sorrows, our fears.

Why?

It was, the scriptures tell us, "that his bowels may be filled with mercy, according to the flesh, that he may know according to the flesh how to succor his people according to their infirmities" (Alma 7:12).

If ever there was a time when we suffer infirmities, it is today. And, consequently, if ever there was a time when we needed to be succored as a result of those infirmities, it is today.

Many understand that *to succor* means to comfort, to bear up, to relieve, to help, to assist—especially in times of distress. For any of us, that would seem to be enough. But *to succor* also means *to run to the aid of.* Can we imagine, then, that in a very real scenario, the Savior waits anxiously *to run to* our aid? There is nothing halfhearted or casual about His offer of help: He is *running* to us, desiring to bring us all the comfort and peace we could ever yearn for or imagine.

He paved the way in Gethsemane. In an agony unimaginable to us, He paid the price so that He *could* be with us—could *run to us*—in our very personal Gethsemanes. He knows those Gethsemanes well, because He went there for us. He knows exactly and precisely how to comfort us in our very personal and individual trials, because He, too, has borne them.

His comfort will ease our suffering. Remember the time during which Alma and his people were in bondage to the Lamanites? Forbidden to pray under threat of death, they "did not raise their voices to the Lord their God, but did pour out their hearts to him; and he did know the thoughts of their hearts" (Mosiah 24:12).

The Lord responded to them as He will respond to us: "the voice of the Lord came to them in their afflictions, saying: Lift up your heads and be of good comfort . . ." (Mosiah 24:13). And while they were not immediately delivered from bondage, He promised them that He would "ease the burdens which are put upon your shoulders, that even you cannot feel them upon your backs, even while you are in bondage" so that the people could "know of a surety that I, the Lord God, do visit my people in their afflictions" (Mosiah 24:14). And that is exactly what happened.

We are told that "it came to pass that the burdens which were laid upon Alma and his brethren were made light; yea, the Lord did strengthen them that they could bear up their burdens with ease, and they did submit cheerfully and with patience to all the will of the Lord" (Mosiah 24:15).

Will our own burdens be immediately lifted? Will our own losses be immediately restored? Will we be immediately freed from the bondage that our difficult times thrust upon us? Those miracles might take place. But if they are delayed, we can be assured—just as the people of Alma still labored under their bondage—that our "burdens may be light, through the joy of his Son" (Alma 33:23), even the Lord Jesus Christ. And, like Alma and his people, we too will, according to His due time, be freed from bondage, from tribulation, from affliction, from pain, from fear. There will come the promised restoration of all things, through Him who is uniquely qualified to restore. Of that we can be certain.

We are, indeed, living through difficult times. We know them to be part of mortality. As we cry out for the comfort we so desperately need in these difficult times, we may fail to see with our mortal vision the blessing in what seems to be such difficulty. The glory of it all is in the journey. The blessing of it all is in what we learn and become along the way. The unparalleled joy of it all is the relationship we develop with the Lord who saves us—who, in all truth, is the only anchor we need.

As we thrash about in perilous times, He is the divine anchor that keeps us safe—safer than any mortal anchor ever could. And His comfort is there for the taking, free to those who bring Him no more than a broken heart and a contrite spirit. We can cry to Him for help and comfort and peace, countless times a day if we need to, and He will always be there, patiently listening, willing to deliver the sought-after calm. With that knowledge, the tender lyrics of "I Need Thee Every Hour" (see *Hymns,* 98) take on a sweet and deeply personal meaning.

Peace and comfort can be ours today. The Lord, who descended below all things so He could run to us in this very moment, brings us that peace and comfort. Looking back on this time—as unimaginable as it seems right now—we will be grateful for the difficulty of these times because of what we will become in the process. We will become His. We will become believers who travel our path with peace, with grace, and with a singleness of vision that brings us sweetly into the arms of a loving Savior who paved the path before us.

Encircled in the comfort of His arms, we will discover in mortality a refuge where we at last find peace.

HEALING THE BLIND MAN

HEALING THE WOUNDED SOUL

JACK R. CHRISTIANSON

"And it supposeth me that they have come up hither to hear the pleasing word of God, yea, the word which healeth the wounded soul."
(Jacob 2:8)

All people, at some point in their lives, are confronted by heartache, tragedy, disappointment, or rejection. I have never known anyone who has not encountered difficulty in their life. It is imperative to our success in mortality that we learn about the Savior and His role as healer. It is imperative because, as Helaman 5:12 informs us, it is not a matter of *if* the devil will attack, but only a matter of *when*. We read that "the devil shall send forth his mighty winds, yea, his shafts in the whirlwind, [and] all his hail and his mighty storm shall beat upon [us]."

Those storms and winds may take the form of divorce, death, contention, sin, disappointment, letdowns, and anything else that would weigh heavily upon us. Helaman 5:12 also gives us some instruction on how to weather these storms. We learn that our foundation must be built upon the rock of Christ so that when the storms arrive, whatever the storm may be, we will not experience the "gulf of misery and endless wo because of the rock upon which ye are built, which is a sure foundation, a foundation whereon if men build they cannot fall."

This verse is not a guarantee that we will escape all difficulty, heartache, or sadness as a reward for doing everything correctly. It does not promise us a life of luxury or ease as a reward for keeping all the commandments of God. However, it does promise us that we *cannot* fall and we will not be miserable and filled with woe.

The word *woe* is defined as "sadness" or "sorrow." In other words, Helaman 5:12 is telling us that if we build the foundation of our lives, marriages, families, and so on upon the foundation of Christ, we will not be dragged down into the gulf of misery and endless "sadness" or "sorrow." Remember, the foundation built upon the rock of Christ is a "sure foundation, a foundation whereon if men build they cannot fall."

"HE HEALED THEM ALL"

We all have heartache, we all have wounds, and we all have pain; therefore, each of us needs to find a way to be healed. The Savior is the key to such healing. Elder Dallin H. Oaks began his October 2005 general conference address with these words:

> Many carry heavy burdens. Some have lost a loved one to death or care for one who is disabled. Some have been wounded by divorce. Others yearn for an eternal marriage. Some are caught in the grip of addictive substances or practices like alcohol, tobacco, drugs, or pornography. Others have crippling physical or mental impairments. Some are challenged by same-gender attraction. Some have terrible feelings of depression or inadequacy. In one way or another, many are heavy laden. . . .
>
> The scriptures contain many accounts of the Savior's healing the heavy laden. . . . Jesus healed many from physical diseases, but He did not withhold healing from those who sought to be "made whole" from other ailments. . . . Great multitudes followed Him, and He "healed them all" (Matt. 12:15). Surely these healings included those whose sicknesses were emotional, mental, or spiritual. He healed them all. ("He Heals the Heavy Laden," *Ensign,* Nov. 2006, 6)

Jesus healed them all! He is a healer of wounded souls, bodies, minds, and hearts—every element involved in the human experience.

FINDING HEALING "IN THE MIDST OF MEDITATION"

As I was pondering these doctrines concerning healing, my mind was drawn to a verse of scripture, Joseph Smith—History 1:44. Joseph was writing about his experience with the angel Moroni. Joseph said, "I lay musing on the singularity of the scene." The angel Moroni had been instructing Joseph, and now what was Joseph doing? He was pondering upon it; he was thinking about it. The word *musing* means he was thinking deeply about and marveling greatly on what he had been told by this extraordinary messenger.

As I read this account, one line in particular stood out to me. It reads, "When, in the midst of my meditation, I suddenly discovered. . . ." Think of that line for a moment. Joseph was, we assume, lying on his bed musing upon what had just occurred, when his room began again to be filled with light. As I read this account, something profound happened to me. I could not get that line out of my mind: "In the midst of my meditation, I suddenly discovered. . . ." Suddenly discovered what? For Joseph Smith, it was that his room began to fill with light. For me, it was something different.

I found that as I pondered, or meditated, I began to find answers to the questions that flowed through my mind, such as, *How can I help Sister Jones as her stake president? How am I going to deal with this or that heavy situation? What am I going to do to help the young couple who is struggling? How am I going to deal with my grandchild who is having difficulty with some of his emotions? What am I going to do to help him? How do I help my daughter who lives so far away?* Not only did I find answers, but I began to ponder about and ask the right questions. *What can I do to better improve my life? How do I get over resentment and anger?* The questions and the answers flowed as I began to apply the simple phrase, "In the midst of my meditation." I began to understand that as we spend time meditating we will discover what it is we need to do. What we need to change. How we can be healed. How we can help lead others to that healing.

In Doctrine and Covenants 101:16, the Savior counseled, "Therefore, let your hearts be comforted concerning Zion; for all flesh is in mine hands; be still and know that I am God." If one of the prerequisites to knowing the Savior is to "be still," how will we ever come to know Him if we seldom take time to be still or to have quiet moments of pondering or meditation? It becomes more difficult, if not impossible, to know Him without quiet time. It becomes difficult to hear the still, small voice of the Spirit. It is difficult because the Spirit's voice is just that: still and small. (See Dallin H. Oaks, "Teaching and Learning by the Spirit," *Ensign*, Mar. 1997, 7–9.)

How will any of us really come to know Him if we do not take time to feel, ponder, and meditate? If we do not know Him, how will we discover what we need to do, learn, or be? How will we learn to access His healing touch?

In December 2005, President Boyd K. Packer spoke at the graduation ceremony for BYU–Hawaii. Concerning this subject of meditation and pondering, he declared: "These are sobering times. You are going out into a world that is different than the world I faced when I was [nineteen]. . . . You won't survive spiritually unless you know how to receive revelation. . . . I don't know whether you know how to receive revelation, but you won't survive without it." He then talked about how the Old Testament prophet Elijah didn't receive revelation in the wind, thunder, or lightning, but from a still, small voice.

In closing, President Packer said, "It's a noisy world, and you're going to have to learn personally, and privately, and individually that revelation will come when the Lord can speak to our feelings. . . . Go quietly into the world, and quietly about your affairs—learn that in the still, small hours of the morning, the Lord will speak to you. He will never fail to answer your prayers" (Boyd K. Packer, BYU–H Commencement Address, Dec. 17, 2005).

We must take time to be still. To be quiet. We must stop and take time each day from our hectic schedules and allow the still, small voice to settle upon our spirits. And when that occurs, "in the midst of our meditation" we will suddenly discover what is necessary to correct ourselves, deal with a problem, correct others (if that's our responsibility), and many other things that will bring healing to our souls and to the souls of others. I have learned for myself that what President Packer said about this matter is absolutely true. We are not going to survive or find the healing we need if we do not know how to receive revelation.

"A MORE POWERFUL EFFECT . . . THAN . . . ANYTHING ELSE"

Is there a "balm of Gilead" to be found in scripture study, prayer, and meditation? Will drenching ourselves in the living waters of the glorious scriptures really heal us of our wounds? When the spirit of revelation comes upon us, and we discover how to handle our difficulties, will our wounds begin to heal? The answer is a resounding *yes*.

It is significant that it was the prophet Jacob, Laman and Lemuel's younger brother, who taught about the healing effect of God's word on the wounded soul. One of the reasons I find his words so powerful is that Jacob himself suffered many wounds from his own family members. He was, by today's standards, a victim of abuse. This adds great power to his teachings on healing. After everything he went through at the hands of his brothers, he teaches us how to be healed of wounds that have come because of the iniquities and mistreatment of others.

In fact, the well-known Book of Mormon chapter that teaches of our need to have "opposition in all things" is actually an exhortation from Jacob's father, Lehi, encouraging Jacob not to give up because his childhood has been so difficult. It begins, "And now, Jacob, I speak unto you: Thou art my first-born in the days of my tribulation in the wilderness. And behold, in thy childhood thou hast suffered afflictions and much sorrow, because of the rudeness of thy brethren" (2 Ne. 2:1). The word *rude* means "harsh," "coarse," "crude," or "vulgar."

If you're a little boy suffering from the harshness, coarseness, crudeness, and vulgarity of your older brothers, what might happen to your self-worth? What might happen to your view of life? How do you find happiness if you are beaten down verbally, emotionally, or even physically, time after time? Jacob's brothers Nephi and Sam were literally beaten down by Laman and Lemuel until delivered by an angel from God, and it's not hard to imagine that at some point faithful Jacob could have met the same fate himself. Jacob also suffered indirectly due to the suffering of others. On his family's voyage to the promised land, his mother, Sariah, was on her deathbed with worry over the behavior of her older children and became unable to feed Jacob or his brother Joseph. (See 1 Ne. 18:18–19.)

Lehi says to Jacob, "Nevertheless, Jacob, my first-born in the wilderness, thou knowest the greatness of God; and he shall consecrate

thine afflictions for thy gain. Wherefore, thy soul shall be blessed, and
thou shalt dwell safely with thy brother, Nephi; and thy days shall be
spent in the service of thy God" (2 Ne. 2:2–3). In other words, "Son,
you have been beaten up emotionally, verbally, and in many other ways,
but the Lord has provided a way to overcome this heartache." Then Lehi
teaches that although there must be "opposition in all things" (v. 11),
"redemption cometh in and through the Holy Messiah" (v. 5).

When Jacob succeeds Nephi as prophet, what does he choose to
teach? He teaches us how to be healed from the wounds of life. How
did Jacob learn and understand the healing process? He lived it. He
knew much of what you and I feel because he felt it. He had to overcome the harsh, coarse, crude, and vulgar actions and words of his
older brothers. This must have made for a very difficult home life—
lacking in harmony at times, and full of contention. If his brothers
desired to kill Nephi and Lehi, we can only imagine how they must
have treated Jacob and Joseph. How did Jacob overcome these enormous negative influences that can be so painful and cause such deep
wounds? He focused on the healing power of the word of God.

The word of God is vital in the healing of wounded souls. The
healing balm found in the scriptures and in the words of the prophets
is like no other.

One problem many face in tapping into the power of the scriptures is learning how to incorporate and use the information rather
than simply reading it. "Feast[ing] upon the words of Christ" (2 Ne.
32:3) is far different than simply reading scriptures regularly. The
Lord has said that the entire Church is under condemnation for not
using the scriptures properly. He declared,

> And your minds in times past have been darkened
> because of unbelief, and because you have treated
> lightly the things you have received—
> Which vanity and unbelief have brought the
> whole church under condemnation.
> And this condemnation resteth upon the children
> of Zion, even all.
> And they shall remain under this condemnation
> until they repent and remember the new covenant,

even the Book of Mormon and the former commandments which I have given them, not only to say, but
to do according to that which I have written. (D&C
84:54–57)

The Lord makes it clear that just reading and talking about the
word of God is not enough. We must *do* something with what we
learn and feel. Doing something is one way to lift the condemnation
the Lord speaks of in the Doctrine and Covenants. I often wonder if
part of our condemnation is that we continue to remain wounded,
hurt, and offended by our own actions or the actions of others,
instead of allowing ourselves to experience the liberation that comes
as our wounds are healed by the word of God.

The Prophet Joseph Smith taught a similar concept. He said, "I
told the brethren that the Book of Mormon was the most correct of
any book on earth, and the keystone of our religion, and a man
would get nearer to God by abiding by its precepts, than by any other
book" (*HC*, 4:461). The way to draw nearer to God, which will surely
lead to the healing of wounds, is to "abide" by the precepts of the
book, not just read about them.

In August 2005, President Gordon B. Hinckley made a statement
about the power of the Lord's words. He asked every Church member
to read the Book of Mormon by the end of that year. With the invitation he gave three promises. "Without reservation I promise you that
if each of you will observe this simple program, regardless of how
many times you previously may have read the Book of Mormon,
there will come into your lives and into your homes an added
measure of the Spirit of the Lord, a strengthened resolution to walk in
obedience to His commandments, and a stronger testimony of the
living reality of the Son of God" ("A Testimony Vibrant and True,"
Ensign, Aug. 2005, 6). Who is the ultimate healer? It is Christ, the
holy Son of God. With these promises in mind, we can even better
understand Nephi's desire for us to come unto the God of Abraham,
Isaac, and Jacob. The intent is for you and I to come to know Him
and then be healed by Him and His word.

What are we waiting for? Why would we not seek the healing that
comes from increasing our testimony of Christ, gaining a stronger

desire to keep the commandments, and having with us a greater portion of the Spirit of the Lord? We have been counseled time and time again to seek the word of God, which "healeth the wounded soul."

In 2005, when members of the Church all over the world began to study and read the Book of Mormon with increased dedication, President Hinckley's three promises began to be fulfilled, and many people experienced a healing in their souls. I saw these promises fulfilled in my own life in great measure. I listened to testimony after testimony of the power of the Book of Mormon in people's lives as they stood at the pulpit and bore witness of the healing balm that it brought. They had greater faith in the reality of the Son of God, they had more strength to resist temptation, and they received a greater measure of the Spirit.

In 1999, Elder Russell M. Nelson spoke about the Book of Mormon in general conference. His message reinforced the principles discussed here. I have used his message many times in counseling and teaching while trying to help individuals experience the Savior's healing power. Elder Nelson said,

> This book can help with personal problems in a very real way. Do you want to get rid of a bad habit? Do you want to improve relationships in your family? Do you want to increase your spiritual capacity? Read the Book of Mormon! It will bring you closer to the Lord and His loving power. He who fed a multitude with five loaves and two fishes—He who helped the blind to see and the lame to walk—can also bless you! He has promised that those who live by the precepts of this book "shall receive a crown of eternal life." (Doctrine and Covenants 20:14; "A Testimony of the Book of Mormon," *Ensign*, Nov. 1999, 71)

According to the title page of the Book of Mormon, the main purpose of the book is to testify of Christ, the Great Healer. Why are so many stories in the scriptures about Jesus' interaction with the wounded, the weary, and the downtrodden? Could it be because of what happens to these people when they come in contact with this Master Healer? When they do, they are healed. The blind see, the deaf hear, the lame walk. We read story after story about Him healing, lifting, nurturing, and loving. What makes the Savior's healing balm so special? It can heal us no matter what our wounds may be. I know this is true.

MEN ARE THAT THEY MIGHT HAVE JOY

The Lord is aware of the problems in the world and even in His Church. But He asks us to remain faithful anyway. Some things will not be cured or fixed in this life, but they will be fixed. Unfortunately, one by-product of wickedness is that it gives the adversary power, at times, in the lives of the afflicted or abused. Yet, the comforting words, "But behold, such shall be reclaimed," offer great healing power. Those who have strayed because of the actions or words of others will, in the end, be reclaimed, and the hypocrites and deceivers will be brought to justice.

The Savior desires to heal all who wish to be healed. In 3 Nephi 17, He is prepared to leave the people of the land of Bountiful and carry on the work of His Father with His other sheep. However, as the Savior looks into these people's eyes, he perceives that they desire Him to stay. The Book of Mormon records,

> And it came to pass that when Jesus had thus spoken, he cast his eyes round about again on the multitude, and beheld they were in tears, and did look steadfastly upon him as if they would ask him to tarry a little longer with them.
>
> And he said unto them: Behold, my bowels are filled with compassion towards you.
>
> Have ye any that are sick among you? Bring them hither. Have ye any that are lame, or blind, or halt, or maimed, or leprous, or that are withered, or that are deaf, or that are afflicted in any manner? Bring them hither and I will heal them, for I have compassion upon you; my bowels are filled with mercy. (3 Ne. 17:5–7)

The Savior not only stayed with the people, but He also healed their sick—and not just the physically sick, but all those "afflicted in any manner."

Before He even appeared to these people, He asked them from the heavens if they would allow Him to be their healer: "O all ye that are spared because ye were more righteous than they, will ye not now return unto me, and repent of your sins, and be converted, that I may heal you?" (3 Ne. 9:13).

Christ is the Great Healer. That is an important part of His mission. He also pleads with God on our behalf and bears testimony to the Father that when His Atonement has taken effect in our lives, we are clean and healed.

In keeping his record, Nephi tells us, "For the fulness of mine intent is that I may persuade men to come unto the God of Abraham, and the God of Isaac, and the God of Jacob, and be saved" (1 Ne. 6:4). Why? Because the God of Abraham, Isaac, and Jacob—Christ—is the true healer of every man, woman, and child.

Mormon wrote that "when he shall appear we shall be like him, for we shall see him as he is" (Moro. 7:48). We shall be like Him because our hearts will be changed; our wounded souls will be made whole. We will stand in the Lord's presence assured of and infinitely grateful in the knowledge that through His merits, we have been redeemed, sanctified, and healed.

JESUS

My Peace I Give Unto You

WAYNE BRICKEY

His Peace Is Different

Just before Jesus entered Gethsemane—the garden that would envelop Him with infinite suffering—He knelt in a crucial, eternity-shaping, high priestly prayer. That prayer marked a shift from His teaching to His atoning. So it is fair to ask what His final themes were before the transition. What messages did the Master save for last? The Apostle John left a record of them. (See John 13–16.)

One message was the last of all. The Savior would speak it to you and me as much as to His eleven friends who hung on every word in their final moments with Him: "These things I have spoken unto you, that in me ye might have peace. In the world ye shall have tribulation: but be of good cheer; I have overcome the world" (John 16:33).

In parting, He spoke of "the world"—a place known for tribulation. (By the way, the word "tribulation" comes from the Latin *tribulo,* meaning to thrash, to pound, to beat up.) Jesus seems to be saying, in His last moment with these men, something like this: "The world will do some pounding on you while you live in mortality. But I invite you, I urge you, I implore you to be of good cheer."

Those who know Him best say that He is "full of grace and truth." The "truth" part of that profile is firm and unvarying. That side of Him takes on the universe and always wins. It makes Him the King. The King has "overcome the world."

But the "grace" side of Him makes Him the Shepherd, the one who personally watches over each soul and sees to each hurt. He, the

One person who is "full of grace," is full of good cheer. (In fact, "grace" and "cheer" derive from the same root.)

Jesus is the pattern of cheer. He is the Source, the "good cheer" leader, you might say. He was that way with His friends just before entering the solemn garden of suffering. When He asked that we be of good cheer, He wasn't commanding; He was radiating it, manifesting it. He was the perfect demonstration. In His voice, in His manner, in His face, were encouragement and assurance.

In the final phrase of that last statement, He talked about the source of His cheer: "be of good cheer; I have overcome the world." He was inviting us to join in His victory over the world, to adopt His burning hope, to be sure of His promises, to be cleansed of fear.

He paid for the great plan and made our perfect brightness of hope perfectly feasible. Our faith permits Him to do with the internal universe what He has done with the external: to still the storms and cause a great calm.

There is something else to notice about the Savior's final message. He linked His peace to all the teachings He had been giving for the preceding hours: "These things I have spoken unto you that ye might have peace."

"These things?" Just what things had He been teaching on that night of nights? John's account gives us more than 120 verses. The lessons are vital, multi-layered and holy—a capstone on the Perfect Teacher's perfect teaching career. But to all of that He assigned this grand purpose: "that ye might have peace."

His truths and promises have a crucial role in our search for His peace. In all our learning of the gospel and all our teaching of it to others, this one outcome is unchanging, like the North Star, and always worthy: *peace*.

In another remark Jesus made earlier that evening, He was already hinting at this hope He has for us—the outcome of peace. And He was careful to say that it isn't just any old peace. "Peace I leave with you, my peace I give unto you: not as the world giveth, give I unto you. Let not your heart be troubled, neither let it be afraid" (John 14:27).

When He promised on another occasion, "I will give you rest," He was not speaking lightly (Matt. 11:28). With His usual good cheer and grace, He was utterly serious.

Clearly, his peace is a gift. We can't create it. And there is nothing else like it. Though He cares about reconciling parties in conflict and rescuing people in distress, His peace is neither of these. Key players in the world, even the best of them, cannot stage or devise it. It isn't a smoothness on the surface of things. It isn't a temporal repair job.

Because this gift is not of our making, and because it is not external, it may be easy to miss. Or underestimate. Or lose. But for these very reasons, it is within our reach. It isn't "out there," but close by, "in here"—in the personal, accessible, internal self. It can be sought and prized and felt and kept forever, by any of us.

GOLIATH VS. PEACE . . . NO CONTEST

We don't have to look very far to find stories of real people blessed with the peace of heaven internally while facing severe difficulties externally. We look at a few examples.

Imagine a young teenaged shepherd named David, asking to fight Goliath. We must go back three thousand years and peek into the tent of King Saul on a small mountain overlooking the Valley of Elah. How might the Lord's peace have affected David and his decisions?

Visualize a large, rectangular tent with a sentry positioned on each of its four sides. Inside, a bodyguard stands at the doorway. At one end, there are two tables, one for meals and the other for writing and holding council. From behind these tables, we are watching this scene.

In the center of the tent sits the king, on a comfortable couch facing the tent opening. The floor around him is covered with rugs, and before him are two small benches for visitors. At the far end of the tent we can see, on a sledlike wooden pallet, a box containing the king's personal weapons and specially fitted pieces of body armor.

King Saul is an imposing man, very tall and well-proportioned, with dark hair and beard, quick eyes, and a kind smile when he chooses to display it. Before him, seated on one of the benches, is fifteen-year-old David, who has just informed Saul that he can defeat Goliath.

Saul asks, "What makes you so sure?"

David answers, "The same thing that has always guided me, that always makes me sure." Without taking his eyes off the king's face,

David raises his hand, slowly makes a fist, and places it against his chest. "A strong peace, in here."

The king pauses, finally nods, and asks, "But how? How would you defeat the Philistine?"

"I will defeat him with precision, from a distance."

"But, my boy, don't you know how big this man is?"

"I have seen him in the valley," David says. He stands, turns in the direction of the tent opening, and points to a spot in the valley where the giant is just barely visible. "There he is now."

The king doesn't bother to look, and motions David to take his seat again. "The man you see is almost a mile away. Up close, it is different. It would not be like facing a man."

"I have faced more than men," David says.

"What do you mean?"

"On one occasion, a bear. Another time, a lion. I killed them." David quickly describes how he defeated those vicious, raging beasts. "God put into my heart then what I feel now. I was guided, and I was not afraid."

The king smiles, "You don't seem afraid now, either."

"I'm not," David says. "But it isn't me. It's not that I was so brave then, or that I am so brave now. It's the peace."

The king sits back on his couch, considers that, and leans forward again with energy. "What if I told you that the huge creature out there—this Goliath—throws a spear as heavy as a man?"

David blinks as he tries to imagine such a thing. That is indeed heavy for one man's tool of battle.

"Think of it, David. Think of this giant who could just as easily, with one of his massive hands, pick up my bodyguard here, as pick up his spear. Or," Saul adds with a smile, "pick up . . . me."

The king chooses to rise from his couch and stand. This he does slowly, just for effect. It is just as people have said. The great leader is taller, by two hand-widths, than any man David has ever seen. The king looks solemnly out at the valley as he rises, but on reaching his full height returns his gaze to David. The kind smile turns to a grim, warning expression, perhaps a pleading look. Saul continues, "That man—that monster—down there doesn't just pick up his great spear and carry it around, David. He uses it in battle. He swings and thrusts with it. My men have seen him throw it through the air, across a distance, at a target."

"Thank you for warning me, sir," David answers. "But what you say . . . it is interesting of course. And I know it should frighten me. But it doesn't. I'm not troubled by that man, or his spear . . ."

"Or his sword? I could tell you of the sword he wields."

"No, not his sword, and not his big voice that fills the valley with curses."

The king sits down again. He thinks for a long while.

David breaks the silence. "You have nothing to lose," he says.

The king looks up and turns his head slightly, inviting David to say more.

"I mean, if I were to die, it wouldn't make matters any worse for the armies of Israel. I'm not a member of your army. The Philistines will know I'm not old enough just by looking at me. If I, a mere boy of Israel, were to die at Goliath's hands, his wager would still be waiting."

"I suppose that is true," Saul concedes. "But, we would lose *you*, David. *That* would be a loss indeed."

"You will not lose anything or anyone. Not even one so insignificant in Israel as myself. I will not die at that man's hands."

Saul leans back again and sighs. "Well, there is one last thing for us to do before I decide about your offer . . . Let's have you try on my armor and heft my sword."

The guard, who has followed every word of this conversation, is visibly puzzled. No one touches the king's personal possessions, least of all his specially crafted weapons and the armor fitted to his frame and skill. The guard wonders if this is a jest of some kind.

David wonders the same thing. Try on the king's armor? For what reason?

Whatever the reason, it is no jest. Without hesitation, the king walks to the far end of the tent and pulls the pallet of battle gear closer to David's bench.

"Here. Put these on."

David obeys. It takes some help from the king and the bodyguard to get the straps right. The breastplate is too wide for David, poking out and restricting the movement of his arms. The lower leggings are too long for his shins, pinching into his ankles. David has never held a full-sized sword before, and this one is oversized. It hangs awkwardly from his grip. When the gear is fully mounted on the boy, the guard is smiling, sure now that David is out of place among trained soldiers.

The king is not smiling. It is as if he is teaching a hard lesson to a promising but naive member of his kingdom, perhaps for some future role.

"You see," the king explains as he looks down into David's eyes, "the battle may belong to you someday. You will wear and wield such things as these in due time. You will slay our enemies as you did the lion and the bear. But can you see that the time for that is not now? You cannot mount the back of Goliath as you did the lion. You cannot cause a paralyzing pain in Goliath's side, or cut the cords in Goliath's neck, as you did the bear. You'll never get that close to him. His armor against yours, his sword against yours . . . don't you see? You will never get within striking range. There is a circle of death around that man, a circle you cannot penetrate."

Still standing awkwardly in the armor and with the sword hanging motionless at his side, David speaks calmly. "You are right about the circle. And you are right about these tools, my king. I'm not ready for them."

David sets the weapons back on the wooden pallet and has help getting unburdened of the larger sections of armor. Only the armplates and leggings remain, for these can be unstrapped without assistance. The king takes his seat again, and the bodyguard moves back to his watchful place by the tent door.

The guard senses that they have done something important here, for you can't just dismiss the courage and faith of this shepherd. He is an Israelite of the true stripe. One should take note of this Bethlehemite. If he can only survive his bold adventures, this brave boy will grow to be a brave man.

The king, refreshed by the clear eyes and pure intent of his student, is poised to excuse him now, and turn his thoughts back to the problematic valley below.

While the audience of two is mentally migrating to other matters, David's mind has not shifted at all. "You have taught me well, my king," he begins. "I am wiser than when I came into your presence. Only one thing remains the same . . ."

Saul nods and waits courteously for David to complete this thought.

"I came here certain that I should meet the giant in battle." David's eyes blaze up and his jaw is set. "Now I know it more surely. You have taught me how *not* to do it. Not with untried implements. I have other armor, and other weapons."

The guard suddenly realizes that there is an extraordinary feeling in this boy's presence, especially when he speaks out of his certainty. It is a warm peace, a deep security, a canceling of fear and confusion. The feeling is now even stronger than before. Saul notices it too.

"So, my king, let me go against him, today—now," David says. "Please." (For the account of David facing Goliath, see 1 Sam. 17.)

REASSURANCES AND FAITH

What was known by one stripling warrior named David was perfectly familiar to a whole army of young men like him centuries later. That familiar sensation was the peace of heaven. *Not instead of trouble, but in the midst of trouble.* Helaman, who saw the timeless miracle again and again with his own eyes, and felt it again and again with his own soul, described it this way:

> We did pour out our souls in prayer to God, that he would strengthen us and deliver us out of the hands of our enemies. . . . And it came to pass that the Lord our God did visit us with assurances that he would deliver us; yea, insomuch that he did speak peace to our souls, and did grant unto us great faith, and did cause us that we should hope for our deliverance in him. (Alma 58:10–11; see also Alma 53 and 56–58)

We know how things turned out for David, and how things turned out for the stripling warriors and their righteous comrades. But when we have the experience ourselves, when we walk where they walked, we discover that the end of the story isn't necessarily the best part. God is willing to "visit us with assurances," and "speak peace to our souls" at the beginning and through the middle of the story as well.

His peace can carry us through the whole plot, whatever the story may be. We are not just slogging along, resigned to the fact that "in the world ye shall have tribulation." During the whole journey, we rejoice to know that "after much tribulation come the blessings" (D&C 58:3–4).

God's reassurances are spoken to the spirit self. We pay Him our ultimate compliment when we simply believe those messages. It is then that the peace grows and radiates out to others.

That compliment—our childlike, uncomplicated trust in His promises—is mighty faith. It is not faith with tortured white knuckles or twisted brow. It is faith that believes the peace, becomes accustomed to it, and lets it grow.

Mighty faith—staying true to the peace, and moving through the middle of the story without swerving or murmuring—is sometimes manifest in a simple smile during setbacks. We have seen that smile on the countenances of living prophets and Apostles as they move through their exhausting schedules and face the unrelenting demand for weighty decisions. The warrior-prophets in history illustrate that trusting willingness to fight battles on one hand, while on the other hand being ever mindful of the glorious outcome.

We think of Joseph Smith, Thomas S. Monson, Moses, and all the others who have kept their headlong pace with poise and peace, and who carried that wonderful countenance of good cheer. The smile of faith and peace doesn't occur because the face is specially equipped or the brain specially designed. No, it is faith that has always kept the Lord's best friends even and kind, steady and unhurried, practical and yet peaceful in the heat of the battle. Faith transforms them into giants of the modest and cheerful variety.

Our times need quiet giants. We need them everywhere, not just in the leading quorums of the Church. Does this call for a work ethic? Of course. Steady, efficient scheduling? By all means. But above all, it calls for a lived-for, prayed-for, heaven-borne peace—its happiness, confidence, balance, and calm radiating from inside the quiet giants.

Once again, the word *grace* comes to mind. Our favorite giants radiate peace in tribulation. There is a sweet absence of fear, fury or flurry, haste or worry. Instead of anxiety, there is grace.

EXAMPLES OF HIS PEACE

Heaven is always ready to comfort those who may never be famous. At any given moment, we can safely assume that trusting, receptive people all over the earth are holding up and being of good cheer because of Christ's light speaking peace to them. By the millions, these toil on through every minute of daylight or lamplight, planting their fields, delivering their papers, caring for the ill in their families, believing all the effort is worth it. They are right, but they have no idea just what a bargain they will gain from their patience and good cheer.

At the end of each faithful person's story, things always work out. The faithful are sure of that guarantee. Certainty opens their inner ears to the steady, pulsing whisper all the way through the story.

As an expert on peace, Gordon B. Hinckley would say: "Things will work out. If you keep trying and praying and working, things will work out. They always do" (Sheri L. Dew, *Go Forward with Faith: The Biography of Gordon B. Hinckley* [Salt Lake City: Deseret Book], 1996, 423). "If you keep trying and praying and working," you can skip over the worrying part. No need to be terrorized by what the scoreboard says. The ending will be triumphant. The game is won from the start. Knowing this, and living this way, we invite the peace of heaven.

Heaven reassures those who are yet without the gospel fullness. That is clear from stories that echo from every neighborhood and lineage on our planet. A small Egyptian man named Gad could spend hours with us, describing the courage and cheer of his loved ones and fellow-villagers. He might even describe how his own little daughter died in his arms several years ago. With her last breath, she pled, "Don't forget me . . . Daddy, will you keep our family together until I see you again?" When he promised he would, she smiled and became still. Those words, a message from heaven sent through a pure child, have kept Gad going day after day. "I loved my daughter so much," he says. "When she died I wanted to die too. But instead, my love for her keeps me going. I must love my son and my wife, I must earn a living and be happy for them. That is how I will keep my promise."

The peace and its good cheer kept things going in Valley Forge. It wasn't enough for a commanding officer named Washington to be steadied by a peace within. The whole valley, filled as it was with snow and hunger, had to be filled with peace in many hearts. Every nation has such heroes, stories of history-making bearers of inspired optimism.

Such stories, from those who have yet to receive the gift of the Holy Ghost, are countless. So, think of the blessed difference it makes to have that Gift—a godly companionship unbroken, ongoing testimony and peace, from a living God. The following words from President Brigham Young will ring true to those who have the gift and have cultivated it:

> You that have not passed through the trials and perse-cutions . . . may think how awful they were to endure, and wonder that the saints survived them at all. The thought of it makes your heart sink within you, . . . and you are ready to exclaim, "I could not have endured it." I have been in the heat of it, and never felt better in all my life; I never felt the peace and power of the Almighty more copiously poured upon me than in the keenest part of our trials. (Brigham Young, in *Deseret News Weekly,* 24 Aug. 1854, 83. Cited by Elder L. Aldin Porter, "But We Heeded Them Not," *Ensign,* Aug. 1998, 6)

The heritage of the faithful is, above all, a gift packaged with peace. And it is more generously poured out "in the keenest part of our trials."

THE SIGNAL

A "signal" is a condensed form of communication, a simple sign that gives immediate meaning. We don't often use the word "signal" to describe something as non-technical as the promptings of the Spirit. But notice this statement from the Lord Himself in a revelation to Joseph Smith and his brethren: "Tarry in this place and in the regions round about; And the place where it is my will that you should tarry, for the main, shall be *signalized* unto you by the peace and power of my Spirit, that shall flow unto you" (D&C 111:7–8; emphasis added). To let these men know where to tarry, the Lord would communicate by a signal of peace and power.

The unique peace of Jesus Christ is distinct from all other sensations—a spiritual signal. It fills our inner selves and carries us gracefully through our dramas. The noticeable flow of His "peace and power" is the way to be sure of His approval. It is the perfect medium of communication from Him to us.

One teacher shared this experience: "In the noisy byways of old Jerusalem, my wife and I once wondered how Jesus ever got the attention of people there. After all, it was as busy and loud then as it is now. It was worth an experiment, so I got up on a big rock in the sheep market and yelled to those nearby. I hardly stirred up a glance, and certainly not an audience. After my wife forgave me for embarrassing her in public, we discussed the experiment and decided that however Jesus got their attention, it wasn't by turning up the volume. It must have been a spiritual power in His words that brought quiet to the crowds. Screaming at people would just not have been His way. And in the Middle East, it wouldn't have worked anyway."

There are those who don't yet seek His peace and are not presently friendly to Him. To these, His special signal is uninteresting and unnoticeable. To those who seek Him, it doesn't need to be loud. For a signal so quiet and simple, it certainly fills a lot of needs. This is how Heber J. Grant described its effects:

> His peace will ease our suffering, bind up our broken hearts, blot out our hates, engender in our breasts a love of fellow men that will suffuse our souls with calm and happiness. (*Teachings of Presidents of the Church: Heber J. Grant*, 219)

Comfort—a healed and softened heart, love, calmness, happiness—that is quite a signal. So, we are not satisfied to keep it to ourselves.

The Savior said, "I give unto you to be the light of the world" (JST Matt. 5:16). He surely doesn't intend His circuitry—His broadcasting system, His signal lights to the world—to keep the signal to themselves. The very "founder" of that peace invites none other than you and me to "publish" it for him. (See 3 Ne. 12:9, 14; Isa. 52:7; 1 Ne. 13:37; Mosiah 15:14–17; Mosiah 27:37; 3 Ne. 20:40.)

BLESSED ARE THE PEACEMAKERS

The phrase "his peace" appears almost countless times in the written words of ancient and modern prophets. In most instances, it is not merely referring to what a prophet enjoys in his own life. It is what he earnestly invokes upon others. Here are just a few echoes from hundreds of prophets and Apostles:

> And now, may the peace of God rest upon you, and upon your houses and lands, and upon your flocks and herds, and all that you possess, your women and your children, according to your faith and good works, from this time forth and forever. (Alma 7:27)

> May his peace and contentment abide in every home. (David O. McKay, *Man May Know for Himself: Teachings of President David O. McKay*, comp. Clare Middlemiss, 430)

> May the Lord add His blessing; may His peace be upon all Israel. (George Albert Smith, *CR*, Oct. 1912, 118)

> May the Lord bless you, my brethren and sisters, and may His peace be upon Zion and her people, and upon all the earth, I pray in the name of Jesus Christ. Amen. (George F. Richards, *CR*, Apr. 1916, 112)

> May God bless you, my wonderful, faithful associates, in this great work. May His peace and His love be upon you and enshrine your lives with an essence of godliness. (Gordon B. Hinckley, "Let Us Live the Gospel More Fully," *Ensign*, Nov. 2003, 102)

OUR BID FOR PEACE

The Prince of Peace provides the lion's share of peace. He paid for it. But there are small things we can do to prepare the way for His enormous role: a soft answer, a tranquil voice, entertainment that is "of good report or praiseworthy," pleasant surroundings, upbeat conversation, inviting interactions. Human beings are more likely to detect and love the voice of Christ when they feel they are treated with decency and dignity and grace. Peacemakers are good at discerning what is necessary and what is not.

Pressure and chaos don't match well with the spirit of peace. We can't imagine them prevailing in the house of the Lord. They don't radiate from Him or lead to Him. In our humble bid for peace—in our awkward effort to at least open a path for Him to enter our souls—we know there are some things to avoid, and some things to foster.

Our bid for peace is foiled by hurry and panic, fear and doubt, rashness and harshness, anger and disputation, dishonesty and overbearance, materialism and greed, pride and ego. It is blocked if we care too much about the things of the world or too little about the people who live in it. These obstruct His way into the hearts of men.

One of those obstacles is hurry. Naturally, it is allied with other obstacles such as fear, doubt, and greed. This calls to mind some counsel from Brigham Young. He was a renowned peacemaker, known for the calm that radiated from him. People felt encouraged when they were open to the influence that flowed from the Lord through this prophet. Behind the calm was the way he lived his faith. That way is available to every peacemaker. He spoke of it in these words:

> This is the counsel I have for the Latter-day Saints today. . . . Do not be in a hurry. . . . You are in too much of a hurry; you do not go to meeting enough, you do not pray enough, you do not read the Scriptures enough, you do not meditate enough, you are all the time on the wing, and in such a hurry that you do not know what to do first. . . . Let me reduce this to a simple saying—one of the most simple and

homely that can be used— 'Keep your dish right side up,' so that when the shower of porridge does come, you can catch your dish full. (*Teachings of Presidents of the Church: Brigham Young,* 235)

We only need to keep our inner selves faced toward the Source. Then, the peace He pours in—a taste of that joy that abides in his own great heart—is plenty and to spare. With that fullness in us, His grace is sufficient for our most difficult days. And there will be extra in our dish to share with the hungry around us.

THE GOOD SHEPHERD

PRINCIPLES AND FEELINGS

C. MAX CALDWELL

The events of these days create chaos and great turmoil in the lives of many people. With a seemingly increasing frequency, these last several years have been filled with one disaster after another, some natural and some man-made. With some regularity, there have been terrible earthquakes causing heavy death tolls and widespread destruction. We remember the mammoth tsunami in the Western Pacific, along with tornados, tropical storms, and hurricanes that have caused a monumental loss of life. Our country, so long a sanctuary from invasion by foreign powers, has been the target of terrorists who have no respect for human life and property. As a result, our country has been thrust into wars in foreign lands along with constant interruptions to our tranquility at home. Nearly every newscast contains reports of never-ending incidents where people suffer at the hands of other human beings.

Our economic world is under siege for various reasons, two primary ones being greed and dishonesty. These qualities have become increasingly visible in the lives of people who could have been such a positive influence for good in the same financial world had they, instead, developed and cultivated traits of honesty, integrity, and selflessness. But now, inestimable numbers of people are suffering the consequential aftermath of lost homes, jobs, and, most importantly, hope.

Even more serious than these destructive forces are the spiritually decimating fruits sown in temptation of which so many people partake.

The Apostle Paul referred to the conditions of our day as "perilous times" (see 2 Tim. 3:1). He was right. Clearly, we face perils of entrapment by insidious snares of sin that are even more harmful to us and our spiritual well-being than the physical challenges we encounter.

With all these unsettled and even sometimes volatile conditions, what should we do to find internal security and emotional relief? The Lord does not want His covenant children to flounder in fear or be discouraged by the dismal views that remain when horizons of hope sometimes fade into disappearing delusions. When so much about us seems to be unsteady and unpredictable, there is, thankfully, a viable and firm foundation upon which we can structure our lives. Though we cannot expect immunity from the hazards of our mortality, we can expect to obtain the strength to withstand trials, resist individual temptation, and overcome consequences of satanically guided influences. Our faith, coupled with confident attitudes, enables us to develop the enthusiasm to endure—and we can personally access a sure source of comfort and peace in our deeply troubled world. That never-failing source is described in the following revealed words of the Savior:

> The works and the designs, and the purposes of God cannot be frustrated, neither can they come to naught.
>
> For God doth not walk in crooked paths, neither doth he turn to the right hand nor to the left, neither doth he vary from that which he hath said, therefore his paths are straight, and his course is one eternal round.
>
> Remember, remember that it is not the work of God that is frustrated, but the work of men. (D&C 3:1–3)

When we walk with the Lord in His paths and struggle to share His strength, we are assured of a steady journey and a divinely designed destination. We are comforted in knowing there is a way. Naturally the question is raised, "How do we find His path and obtain His strength?"

The answer seemed to leap out at me as I was recently completing another reading of the Book of Mormon. In an epistle to his son, Moroni, the prophet Mormon was describing many of the degenerate practices and depraved conditions of his people. He then wrote a concluding statement identifying the cause of their wickedness. He stated "they are without *principle,* and past *feeling . . .*" (Moro. 9:20).

We note that the absence of these two qualities in a people resulted in their lives being mired in the mud of misery. Essentially they had no standards and no sense of wrongdoing. They were far, far away from the Savior's path and plan of happiness and yet completely lacking in desire to make changes. They were apparently unaware of the reason they were in such a state. If they ever knew, they obviously had forgotten the declaration of Isaiah, "There is no peace, saith the LORD, unto the wicked" (Isa. 48:22).

Given the condition of the people because they lacked principles and feelings, we can conclude that when people *do* possess those two attributes, they will enjoy conditions of peace.

Remember the words of the Savior following His Resurrection and appearance to the Nephites. He provided them with an eternal perspective and promise in the following commandment which, if kept, would assure them of peace and prosperity and preclude their falling into the state of misery eventually experienced by their posterity centuries later. He said, "And ye see that I have commanded that none of you should go away, but rather have commanded that ye should come unto me, that ye might *feel* and *see*" (3 Ne. 18:25; emphasis added).

The Savior promised two attainable qualities to those who come unto Him: They will be able to *feel* and to *see.* Each of these senses has two dimensions—one external, or physical, and the other internal. Externally, these two physical senses make it possible for us to feel when we touch tangible things and to see tangible things as they come into our view. This promise was fulfilled for 2,500 people at the temple in Bountiful when

> the multitude went forth, and thrust their hands into
> [the Savior's] side, and did feel the prints of the nails
> in his hands and in his feet; and this they did do,

going forth one by one until they had all gone forth,
and *did see with their eyes and did feel with their hands,*
and did know of a surety and did bear record, that it
was he, of whom it was written by the prophets, that
should come. (3 Ne. 11:15; emphasis added)

We experience many kinds of *feelings* internally. Generally
speaking, in the scriptures the heart is considered to be a depository
of feelings. As an example, love is a feeling the Lord commands us to
have for Him, and we are to do so with all our heart (see D&C 59:5).
A testimony is a feeling that comes as the Holy Ghost bears witness of
truth to our soul. Moroni promised that "by the power of the Holy
Ghost ye may know the truth of all things" (Moro. 10:5). And how
will we know? The Lord promised that as we pray to know what is
true, "your bosom shall burn within you; therefore, you shall *feel* that
it is right" (D&C 9:8; emphasis added).

"Seeing" things internally equates with the process of understanding. Early in His ministry the Savior told Nicodemus, ". . .
Except a man be born again [of the water and the Spirit], he cannot
see the kingdom of God" (John 3:3, emphasis added). In other words,
one can only understand or comprehend the teachings and principles
of truth taught by the Savior and His authorized representatives when
they are listening or reading under the influence of the Holy Spirit. In
our dispensation, the Savior declared, "Wherefore, he that preacheth
and he that receiveth [by the Spirit], understand one another, and
both are edified and rejoice together" (D&C 50:22; see also
50:10–25). Or as Nephi taught, "For the Lord God giveth light unto
the understanding; for he speaketh unto men according to their
language, unto their understanding" (2 Ne. 31:3).

We should remember that the privilege of having these feelings
and insights as identifiers of right and truth is a blessing that comes to
those who come unto Christ and receive the witness of the Spirit and,
if baptized, the gift of the Holy Ghost. The Holy Spirit also then
provides a wide array of gifts to those who are worthy recipients. The
Apostle Paul counseled the Ephesian Saints to not be as the Gentiles,
"Having the *understanding* darkened, being alienated from the life of
God through the ignorance that is in them, because of the blindness

of their heart: Who being *past feeling* have given themselves over unto lasciviousness" (Eph. 4:18–19; emphasis added). We remember that Nephi chastised his brothers, "Ye are swift to do iniquity but slow to remember the Lord your God. Ye have seen an angel, and he spake unto you; yea, ye have heard his voice from time to time; and he hath spoken unto you in a still small voice, *but ye were past feeling, that ye could not feel his words*" (1 Ne. 17:45; emphasis added).

It is incumbent upon each of us to focus on the ways of Christ, from whom comes revealed principles with accompanying feelings of peace. We need to read and listen to the Lord's words as written or proclaimed by His spokesmen, even prophets of God. Joseph Smith taught that "Faith comes by hearing the word of God, through the testimony of the servants of God; that testimony is always attended by the Spirit of prophecy and revelation" (Joseph Fielding Smith, comp., *Teachings of the Prophet Joseph Smith* [Salt Lake City: Deseret Book Company], 1976, 148).

When the word of the Lord is spoken, the power of the witness generated by the Holy Spirit is carried "unto the hearts of the children of men" (2 Ne. 33:1). The subsequent feelings are settling to the soul while creating motivational desires to live by the principles being taught. No wonder the Lord was so emphatic when He declared: "I have commanded you to bring up your children in light and truth" (D&C 93:40).

The message for all of us is we should not dwell on, expand visibility of, nor provide any form of support to the evil ways of our society and our world. We should not expose our families or our people to the various manifestations of evil so easily found all around us. Some rationalize that our people need to experience the ways of the world in order to recognize and be prepared to cope with such worldliness. The obvious hazard in that approach is that the Holy Spirit does not participate in unholy ways or dwell in unholy places. By our doing so, we alienate ourselves from the Spirit and are without the uplifting power we otherwise could have.

A better course for us would be to follow the teaching pattern the Lord used with Moses. The Lord provided him with a marvelous spiritual experience. Moses felt the power and glory of the Lord upon him while being taught. Then when Lucifer appeared to Moses, tempting him, Moses was able to notice the absence of glory associated with Lucifer, and thus discern the difference in what he saw and felt, thereby detecting the deceiver, and separating himself from his evil presence. (See Moses 1:1–22.)

The lesson is clear. All of us need to be engaged in learning and living divine principles under the influence of the Holy Spirit, thereby increasing our ability to discern truth from error.

As we mentioned before, the Lord's people are not to be shielded from the vicissitudes of life. Unless we encounter opposition we do not struggle, and if we do not struggle we do not increase in strength. The prophet Alma knew that was part of the Lord's plan for us, but that we would not need to struggle alone if we exercised faith in the Lord and His teachings. Alma testified to his son: "And now, O my son Helaman, behold, thou art in thy youth, and therefore, I beseech of thee that thou wilt hear my words and learn of me; for I do know that *whosoever* shall put their trust in God shall be supported in their trials, and their troubles, and their afflictions, and shall be lifted up at the last day" (Alma 36:3; emphasis added).

Alma knew about the Lord's support from his own experience with trials. He recorded, "And I have been supported under trials and troubles of every kind, yea, and in all manner of afflictions; yea, God has delivered me from prison, and from bonds, and from death; yea, and I do put my trust in him, and he will still deliver me" (Alma 36:27).

Some may think his role as a prophet gave him special help from above, but we notice that in his testimony to his son, he used the word *whosoever* to expand the Lord's promise to all who put their trust in him. It is also interesting to remember that our challenges will not be unique; Alma encountered "troubles of every kind . . . and all manner of afflictions." The support promise encompasses all who trust, and has unlimited applicability to every affliction, whether it be economic, health, death, or suffering of any kind.

Alma continued his counsel on these principles by reviewing the experience of Lehi's journey in the wilderness when the families were privileged to be led by the Liahona, which the Lord prepared for them. But it only provided divine guidance

. . . according to their faith in God; therefore, if they had faith to believe that God could cause that those spindles should point the way they should go, behold, it was done . . . [but they] were slothful, and forgot to exercise their faith and diligence and then those marvelous works ceased . . . [they] did not travel a direct course, and were afflicted with hunger and thirst, because of their transgressions. . . . these things are not without a shadow; for as our fathers were slothful to give heed to this compass (now these things were temporal) they did not prosper; even so it is with things which are spiritual. . . . it is as easy to give heed to the word of Christ, which will point to you a straight course to eternal bliss, as it was for our fathers to give heed to this compass. (Alma 37:40–44)

This great prophet's counsel applied to trials that are both temporal as well as spiritual. Almost as a summation statement of principles, Alma delivered this concluding directive: "see that ye look to God and live" (Alma 37:47).

For some, that statement might give rise to a very meaningful question. Most Church members know that Jesus is the reason why we will have life in an immortal and resurrected body. Most of us probably also know that because of the Atonement of Christ we can enjoy life free from the impurities of sin, both here and hereafter. But why is He able to provide for and sustain us here and now while living with trials and afflictions in our mortal lives?

There is a powerful reason behind Alma's last statement to Helaman. He knew that the Son of God would one day be born, grow to manhood, and serve His ministry among the Jews. Alma also knew and had taught that Jesus would face a life of mortality wherein He should

go forth, suffering pains and afflictions and temptation *of every kind;* and this that the word might be fulfilled which saith he will take upon him the pains and the sicknesses of his people.

And he will take upon him death, that he may loose the bands of death which bind his people; and

he will take upon him their infirmities, that his
bowels may be filled with mercy, according to the
flesh, *that he may know according to the flesh how to
succor his people according to their infirmities.*

. . . the Son of God suffereth according to the
flesh that he might [also] take upon him the sins of
his people, that he might blot out their transgressions
according to the power of his deliverance. (Alma
7:11–13; emphasis added)

Jacob also bore witness that the scope of the Savior's mortal
suffering and Atonement would be unlimited for the pains and sins of
all people who would come unto Him. Jacob testified that Jesus would
come "into the world that he may save all men if they will hearken
unto his voice; for behold, he suffereth the pains of all men, yea, the
pains of every living creature, both men, women, and children, who
belong to the family of Adam" (2 Ne. 9:21). Most people know the
Savior bore the burdens of sin for all people, so that all who repent can
be the recipient of His mercy and forgiving powers. But many people
do not know that the Savior also experienced every kind of pain, affliction, and temptation that mortals experience. Truly He could declare,
"The Son of Man hath descended below them all" (D&C 122:8).

In our dispensation, He further taught, "Behold, and hearken, O
ye elders of my church, saith the Lord your God, even Jesus Christ,
your advocate, who knoweth the weakness of man and how to succor
them who are tempted" (D&C 62:1). How comforting it is to realize
the magnitude of the Savior's atoning mission, thereby making it
possible for Him to use His knowledge and powers in our behalf if we
will only hearken to His principles.

As an illustration of how the Lord can help us, we turn to the
time when Joseph Smith wavered in his stewardship responsibility for
the Book of Mormon translation. The Lord chastised him and
reminded him how the problems associated with the loss of the 116
pages of manuscript could have been avoided. The Lord said,

For, behold, you should not have feared man more
than God. Although men set at naught the counsels of

God, and despise his words—Yet you should have
been faithful; and he would have extended his arm
and supported you against all the fiery darts of the
adversary; and he would have been with you in every
time of trouble. (D&C 3:7–8)

We are to liken the scriptures unto ourselves (see 1 Ne.
19:23–24). We learn from the above-quoted verse, then, that we can
also expect the support of the Lord in every time of trouble, if we are
faithful as the Lord expected Joseph to be.

We conclude that the Savior's atoning sacrifice opens comforting
doors for us when we:

1. Need to be released from consequences of sin and be healed of
sin-caused wounds. Those who heed the Lord's invitation to repent
and come to Him receive forgiveness and healing and are blessed with
a peace of conscience illuminated by the light of redemption.

2. Need to be reminded that death is not the end of life for
anyone, but it is a sweet release from physically suffering the trials of
mortality. For those who have hearkened to the gathering voice of the
Savior, death brings a new vista of life in the paradisiacal spirit world
while waiting for the day of the glorious resurrection.

3. Need relief from temporal and temporary burdens. Those who
trust Christ will be supported in their afflictions, their burdens will be
lightened, and their focus will shift from despair to gratitude for the
uplifting and edifying principles of the restored gospel. Whatever
their needs, the Lord knows how to succor them.

When we speak of the need to be gathered unto the Lord, we
should be reminded of the way the Lord gathers His people. He has
said He "will gather his people even as a hen gathereth her chickens
under her wings, even as many as will hearken to my voice and
humble themselves before me, and call upon me in mighty prayer"
(D&C 29:2). Anyone who has watched a mother hen gather her
chicks has noticed that she does not go to the chick and pick it up
with her beak. But at the sign of danger or need for the chicks to
come to their mother, she simply clucks her call and waits for the
chicks to respond. When they come, she nestles them under her wings
and they are safe. The Lord does likewise. He extends His call to all

people and warns them of danger, but He does not go to select individuals to bring them home. Rather, He waits for them to decide if they will hearken and come to Him. While He waits, His "arm is stretched out in the last days, to save [His] people Israel" (D&C 136:22).

The symbolic image of His arm being stretched out has great significance for us. We all remember how He died with arms stretched out and pinned to the cross. In that position He was in pain and still suffering for us. Now we read of His arms being extended towards us with an invitation to come to Him and be welcomed into His arms. Referring to the Lord, Alma taught, "Behold, he sendeth an invitation unto all men, for *the arms of mercy are extended* towards them, and saith: Repent, and I will receive you" (Alma 5:33; emphasis added). The Savior invites and waits with open arms for them to come to Him.

In our dispensation, we see the Lord has not changed, and He looks upon the people of our day the same as all others. To Oliver Cowdery, He said, "Behold, thou art Oliver, and I have spoken unto thee because of thy desires; therefore treasure up these words in thy heart. Be faithful and diligent in keeping the commandments of God, and *I will encircle thee in the arms of my love*" (D&C 6:20; emphasis added).

I will take the liberty of rephrasing a statement made by the prophet Mormon to his son Moroni. I will write it as if he were addressing it to faithful brothers and sisters today who face trials and afflictions in our troubled world, assuring us that we can yet obtain the strength to endure them and find peace from the ultimate source of comfort—the Lord Jesus Christ. Consider these modified verses:

> Behold my beloved brothers and sisters of the latter days. I recommend thee unto God, and I trust in Christ that thou wilt be saved from the destructive forces of worldliness; and I pray unto God that He will spare thy righteous way of life, that you might experience the strength His people receive from Him.
>
> My dear brothers and sisters, be faithful in Christ; and may not the things of the world which threaten

to destroy your faith and your confidence in the ways of the Lord grieve thee, to weigh thee down; but may Christ lift thee up, lighten your burdens, and support you with hope of His glory and of eternal life, and may these promised blessings rest in your mind forever. (See Moro. 9:22, 25)

Now, I would like to share an account of an experience recorded by Melvin J. Ballard, who was subsequently called to be a special witness of Christ and to serve in the Quorum of Twelve Apostles.

Away on the Fort Peck Reservation where I was doing missionary work with some of our brethren, laboring among the Indians, seeking the Lord for light to decide certain matters pertaining to our work there, and receiving a witness from him that we were doing things according to his will, I found myself one evening in the dreams of the night in that sacred building, the temple. After a season of prayer and rejoicing I was informed that I should have the privilege of entering into one of those rooms, to meet a glorious Personage, and, as I entered the door, I saw, seated on a raised platform, the most glorious Being my eyes have ever beheld or that I ever conceived existed in all the eternal worlds. As I approached to be introduced, he arose and stepped towards me *with extended arms,* and he smiled as he softly spoke my name. If I shall live to be a million years old, I shall never forget that smile. He took me *into his arms* and kissed me, pressed me to his bosom, and blessed me, until the marrow of my bones seemed to melt! When he had finished, I fell at his feet, and, as I bathed them with my tears and kisses, I saw the prints of the nails in the feet of the Redeemer of the world. The *feeling* that I had in the presence of him who hath all things in his hands, to have his love, his affection, and his blessing was such that if I ever can receive that of which I had but a foretaste, I would give all that I am, all that I ever hope to be, *to feel what I then felt!*

I see Jesus not now upon the cross. I do not see his brow pierced with thorns nor his hands torn with the nails, but I see him smiling, *with extended arms,* saying to us all; "Come unto me." (*Sermons and Missionary Services of Melvin J. Ballard* [Salt Lake City, Utah: Deseret Book Company, 1949], 156–57; emphasis added)

Though we may not have a physical and personal encounter with heavenly beings, we are all extended the opportunity to come into the spiritual presence of the Savior and receive of His Holy Spirit. From the Holy Ghost we receive insights and understand principles with an accompanying spiritual witness of their truth that creates uplifting and edifying feelings in our heart.

How grateful I am, as all of us can be, for the capacity to feel. We can feel the Lord's love for us and ours for Him and others of His children. We can feel the peace of a cleansed soul concurrently with convictions of conversion. We can feel increased spiritual strength resulting in relief from distress caused by challenging trials common to our mortal existence; we can feel the lightening of the burdens we bear.

We can feel a constant acceptance of a Heavenly Father and His Son providing encouragement to endure when, at the same time, we may be experiencing rejections from an array of other sources. We can feel the joy of partaking of the plan of happiness as we hearken to the word of the Lord that keeps us steady on the straight and narrow path to eternal life. We can feel the indescribable waves of warmth when we accept the invitation of our Master who says, "Come unto me that ye might feel and see" (3 Ne. 18:25).

GETHSEMANE

OUR SHIELD

LEAUN G. OTTEN

At some time in our mortal lives, all of us have experienced rare moments when we find ourselves all alone, when there is no pressure of appointments or work, when no other persons are around us. We are alone—really alone—with only ourselves, reflecting back over the events of our lives, both the good and the undesirable. At that moment, we feel a secret something, a far-off reflection, a familiar spirit signaling that we are strangers on this planet earth; we feel we have come from another abode or sphere, that our stay here is but a small moment in time.

In these sobering, quiet moments, we realize to some extent that we are alone, marooned on this planet with other mortals. Then in total honesty we ask ourselves: *Who am I? Do I really know myself? Do I really know where I came from and why I am here? What is life really about?* Then our minds are caught up to a higher plane of reasoning, touched by an unseen power—and we receive the light of understanding, something innate, a whispering to which our intellect and emotions eagerly respond: There is truly a God in heaven who is our Father; we are His children, and we are loved by Him. We are not alone on planet earth.

Yet, almost immediately, reality again appears on the stage of our minds, revealing our heartaches, our pains, our struggles, our disappointments. Life is not easy; in fact, it is a tough schoolmaster. Everything we choose to do and experience comes with a price and carries with it consequences, either good or bad. Well did the preacher declare:

> To everything there is a season, and a time to every
> purpose under the heaven:
> A time to be born, and a time to die; a time to
> plant, and a time to pluck up that which is planted . . .
> A time to weep, and a time to laugh; a time to
> mourn, and a time to dance . . .
> A time to get, and a time to lose; a time to keep, and
> a time to cast away;
> A time to rend, and a time to sew; a time to keep
> silence, and a time to speak;
> A time to love, and a time to hate; a time of war,
> and a time of peace. (Eccl. 3:1–8)

Most of us have experienced much of the above dramas of life expressed by the preacher. As our reflections upon life's experiences deepen, questions repeatedly consume our minds. *Whom can we ask, speak to, counsel with, and express our concerns about the stresses of life, the heartaches, our disappointments and sorrows? Who has successfully lived mortal life that can and would understand our concerns? Is there anyone we can trust?* The answer to these questions is the most comforting knowledge that mortals can embrace during our earthly sojourn. There is One Being who has graced this mortal earth upon whom we can rely. He experienced and successfully met every challenge and mastered every obstacle befalling mortals. He is the Great I Am, Jehovah, the Prince of Peace, even Jesus Christ. His revealed word from heaven declares that He

> shall dwell in a tabernacle of clay, and shall go forth
> amongst men, working mighty miracles, such as healing
> the sick, raising the dead, causing the lame to walk, the
> blind to receive their sight, and the deaf to hear, and
> curing all manner of diseases. And he shall cast out
> devils, or the evil spirits which dwell in the hearts of the
> children of men. And lo, he shall suffer temptations,
> and pain of body, hunger, thirst, and fatigue, *even more
> than man can suffer.* . . .

> And he shall be called Jesus Christ, the Son of God,
> the Father of heaven and earth, the Creator of all things
> from the beginning. (Mosiah 3:5–8; emphasis added)

He suffered temptations more than man can suffer. He suffered pain of body more than man can suffer. He suffered hunger, thirst, and fatigue more than man can suffer. Why did a Son of God come to mortal earth and experience all the ills of this life, even more than we can experience? We do not know all the reasons. However, from the revealed word of God, we learn some of the purposes of the mission of His Only Begotten Son. Two revealed purposes are paramount.

First: Jesus Christ suffered that He might be able to show mercy and give succor according to our needs. The prophets have recorded:

> And he shall go forth, suffering pains and afflictions and temptations of every kind; *and this that the word might be fulfilled which saith he will take upon him the pains and the sicknesses of his people.*
>
> And he will take upon him death, that he may loose the bands of death which bind his people; and he will take upon him their infirmities, that his bowels may be filled with mercy, according to the flesh, *that he may know according to the flesh how to succor his people according to their infirmities.* (Alma 7:11–12; emphasis added)

> Behold, and hearken, O ye elders of my church, saith the Lord your God, even Jesus Christ, your advocate, *who knoweth the weakness of men and how to succor them who are tempted.* (D&C 62:1; emphasis added)

Yes, there is one, only one perfect person, the Son of a God, who knows how to help us when we suffer both physical and mental anguish, when we experience heartache, when we are tempted, even when we sin. One of the paramount purposes for His mission to this earth was to experience all the ills of the mortal flesh in order to know how to succor or give the merciful comforting aid of which we all stand in need. He and He alone is the great source of comfort for all mankind.

One of the most sublime treatises regarding this great, divine principle is given to us by the prophet Nephi. We are enlightened and feel hope as we walk with Nephi through one of his great disappointments, sorrows, and tests of life. He reached a point in his suffering when he realized that only Jesus Christ could help him, give succor, and offer divine mercy. Following years of abuse from his erring brothers, Laman and Lemuel, and after the death of his father, Nephi yields to the weakness of the flesh and begins to harbor anger, even hatred, towards them. All mankind can identify with Nephi's struggle. He recorded his feelings:

> And why should I yield to sin because of my flesh? Yea, why should I give way to temptations, that the evil one have place in my heart to destroy my peace and afflict my soul? Why am I angry because of mine enemy?
>
> Awake, my soul! No longer droop in sin. Rejoice, O my heart, and give place no more for the enemy of my soul.
>
> Do not anger again because of mine enemies. Do not slacken my strength because of mine afflictions.
>
> Rejoice, O my heart, and cry unto the Lord, and say: O Lord, I will praise thee forever; yea, my soul will rejoice in thee, my God, and the rock of my salvation.
>
> O Lord, wilt thou redeem my soul? Wilt thou deliver me out of the hand of mine enemies. . . ?
>
> O Lord, wilt thou encircle me around in the robe of thy righteousness! . . .
>
> O Lord, I have trusted in thee, and I will trust in thee forever. . . .
>
> Yea, I know that God will give liberally to him that asketh. Yea, my God will give me, if I ask not amiss. (2 Ne. 4:27–31, 33–35)

If there is one lesson that can be learned from Nephi, it is that there is only one ultimate source of understanding, comfort, and peace. This source is Jesus Christ, who knows how to succor mortals. He can heal our sorrows and bring peace to our souls. Mortal man is unable to fully understand Christ's ability to give the comfort and peace so needed by all of us living today—carrying heavy burdens, troubles, sorrows, and heartaches—in such a troubled world. The words of Nephi extend divine hope and comfort to all of us.

Some years ago I was discussing this topic with students I was teaching. Several class periods later a student gave me a letter written by one of his ancestors. He gave me permission to use it in my teachings. This ancestor experienced a failed marriage. Her parents attributed all her troubles, sorrows, and heartaches to her decision to become affiliated with another church. Her letter is an answer to their criticism. Note her source of comfort.

> If you strip everything away from me—everything, and leave the most elemental parts of me that exist, you know what you'll find staring out at you? Somebody who loves the Lord, and is loved back. And that is what makes me run. He loves me—and it is a kind of love that is beyond our conception of love. And it isn't just for me; it's for all of His children. . . . That is the God I've given myself to—and all that I am, all that I hope for and yearn for, all that I treasure—everything that I am or could ever hope to be or have. I give it not always without a few tears, not always as cheerfully as I would like . . . but I give it because I know, I *know* that when He is through with it, He'll give it back, more beautiful, more holy, more full of joy, and more fulfilled than I could have dreamed of making it on my own. Do you see what I'm saying? That is why you're not to feel sorry for me. Does one feel sorry for a lump of clay when the artist begins to mold it? Does one feel pity for the stone when the sculptor chisels and carves away at it? The strokes may hurt me, but just wait till you see what the Artist finishes, when He is finished with me!

Second, Jesus Christ will take away our burdens and sorrow for sin. Mortals grieve and sorrow for two reasons. First, there are physical problems: environmental concerns, adjusting to other people, illness, disappointments, and death. The other source of grief and sorrow is personal sin. Mortals cannot sin against other mortals. We can bring harm to another mortal. We can trespass on their agency, but we cannot sin against them. We can only sin against the Lawgiver, even God our Father and His Only Begotten Son. All mankind are sinners, even when we trespass against our fellowmen.

While carrying our burden of sins we are troubled and have no peace. No mortal being can eradicate our sins and restore divine peace to our souls. Again, only one Being, a sinless Being, has graced mortal earth, experienced all the ills of this life, and with merciful compassion atoned for all our sins, extending peace to our souls. When we understand this divine principle and desire to adhere to the requirements necessary to partake of Jesus Christ's Atonement, we will find peace in a troubled world. President David O. McKay taught this principle when he said: "Men may yearn for peace, cry for peace, and work for peace, but there will be no peace until they follow the path pointed out by the Living Christ" (CR, Apr. 1948, 68). Finding peace requires humble, honest, simple faith in the Lord Jesus Christ, and a hope in His glory, without which nothing changes.

His compassion and love for us is beyond human understanding. He willingly gave His own life so we could rid ourselves of our sins, which bring such sorrow. The message in the following verses is like the dews of heaven distilling upon troubled souls:

> For behold, I, God, have suffered these things for all, that they might not suffer if they would repent;
> Which suffering caused myself, even God, the greatest of all, to tremble because of pain, and to bleed at every pore, and to suffer both body and spirit—and would that I might not drink the bitter cup, and shrink—
> I am Jesus Christ; I came by the will of the Father, and I do his will. (D&C 19:16, 18, 24)

Remember the worth of souls is great in the sight of God;

For, behold, the Lord your Redeemer suffered death in the flesh; wherefore he suffered the pain of all men, that all men might repent and come unto him.

And he hath risen again from the dead, that he might bring all men unto him, on conditions of repentance. (D&C 18:10–12)

Surely he hath borne our griefs, and carried our sorrows. . . .

. . . he was wounded for our transgressions, he was bruised for our iniquities: the chastisement of our peace was upon him; and with his stripes we are healed. (Isa. 53: 4–5)

So simple, so divine, so attainable is the way to secure peace in our souls while living in a troubled world. The Great Prince of Peace, even Jesus Christ, has invited all of us to come unto Him and partake of His peace. "Peace I leave with you, my peace I give unto you: *not as the world giveth, give I unto you.* Let not your heart be troubled, neither let it be afraid" (John 14:27; emphasis added). Through the power of His Atonement, the Savior of all mankind has opened the door of repentance. We receive His grace, mercy, and love for us by repenting of our sins and coming unto Him. Our souls are at peace; our sorrows, heartaches, disappointments, trials, and all other ills of mortal life are understood by Him "who knoweth the weakness of man and how to succor them who are tempted" (D&C 62:1).

To all of us who have received this peace of our Savior Jesus Christ and to all who will obtain this heaven-sent blessing, I testify that we can be protected from yielding to the ills of this troubled world and abandoning our faith in Jesus Christ. What will help us to stay the course each day?

May I suggest the following six simple reminders that are easy to formulate in our minds.

First, pray. Our ultimate shield is Jesus Christ. If we sincerely ask Him to *shield* us from yielding to discouragement and temptation, He has promised to answer our sincere and honest petitions. "My voice shalt thou hear in the morning, O Lord; in the morning will I direct my prayer unto thee, and will look up. . . . For thou, Lord, wilt bless the righteous; with favour wilt thou compass him as with a *shield*" (Ps. 5:3, 12; emphasis added).

Second, keep a high opinion of ourselves. We are the offspring of God. He is our Father. How divine, how secure, how humbling, how inspiring to our souls is this heaven-sent knowledge. The prophet Moses was greatly impressed and inspired after learning that he was a son of God. Responding to Satan's tempting invitation, he said: "Behold, I am a son of God, in the similitude of his Only Begotten; and where is thy glory, that I should worship thee?" (Moses 1:13). This is a great guidepost, a reminder to us as we traverse the path of life each day. We must never forget that we are children of God. We need to keep a high opinion of ourselves. Commenting on this principle, President Harold B. Lee taught,

> A great psychologist, MacDougall, once said: "The first thing to be done to help a man to moral regeneration is to restore, if possible, his self-respect." Also I recall the prayer of the old English weaver, "O God, help me to hold a high opinion of myself." That should be the prayer of every soul; not an abnormally developed self-esteem that becomes haughtiness, conceit, or arrogance, but a righteous self-respect that might be defined as "belief in one's own worth, worth to God, and worth to man." ("Stand Ye in Holy Places," *Ensign*, July 1973, 6–7)

Faith in the fact that God is our Father will inspire each one of us to hold a high opinion of ourselves.

Third, don't look back—look forward. We have come to Christ; we have repented of our sins; we have been forgiven; we have received His peace to our souls. Our merciful God will remember our sins no more. Our transgressions will not be mentioned before the Lord. Then why should we look back? Why should we desire to carry the burdens that have been lifted off our shoulders? Why should we submit to unnecessary pain and sorrow again? All has been taken away in Christ, all has been buried with His death, all has been crucified with Him. All our sins and transgressions have been buried deep in the graveyard of past mistakes through the mercy of Jesus Christ's Atonement.

A great lesson can be learned from a group of people known as the Anti-Nephi-Lehies, who buried from their lives the very things that denied them the peace of Jesus Christ.

> We will hide away our swords, yea, even we will *bury* them deep in the earth, that they may be kept bright, *as a testimony* that we have never used them, at the last day. . . .
>
> And they did *bury* them up deep in the earth.
>
> And this they did, it being *in their view a testimony to God,* and also to men, that they never would use weapons again for the shedding of man's blood; and this they did, vouching and covenanting with God, that rather than shed the blood of their brethren they would give up their own lives. (Alma 24:16–18; emphasis added)

The question all of us have to ask ourselves in all honesty is, do I really love God my Father and Jesus Christ, His Only Begotten Son? Do I love Them enough that I will never look back? Do I love Them enough to leave the past buried and give my all to Him, even my sins and transgressions? We can begin each day with the sweet knowledge and witness that our past sins and transgressions have been *buried* with Him who gave His life for us. We have risen with Him to a new life. We need not look back. Our faith is in Jesus Christ. We love Him. Each day we look forward with hope, peace, and with a covenant and testimony that we will be true to Him.

Fourth, remember that God will give us experience for our good. We live in a temporal (temporary), imperfect, and demanding world. It is filled with sickness, disappointments, heartaches, sorrows—even death. Yet, in spite of these challenging experiences, the Lord has revealed to all of us the purpose of our exposure to all the vicissitudes of life. In the depths of despair while Joseph Smith was incarcerated in a filthy prison, the Lord revealed to him in answer to his pleading the most comforting, enlightening, meaningful, and eternal principles of life. "Thine adversity and thine afflictions shall be but a small moment; And then, if thou endure it well, God shall exalt thee on high; thou shalt triumph over all thy foes. . . . All these things shall give thee experience, and shall be for thy good" (D&C 121:7–8; 122:7).

These principles are vital to our mental and spiritual health. How wonderful it is to be in control when the dramas of life unfold before us, and we can understand that we can be victorious by adhering to this heaven-sent knowledge.

Fifth, know that all good comes from the Lord—and all wickedness comes from the devil. We are not left alone here in mortality to wander helplessly, not knowing good from evil. "Men are instructed sufficiently that they know good from evil" (2 Ne. 2:5). In every culture, mankind knows that stealing, lying, murder, sexual misconduct, and other similar behaviors are wrong. The gospel of Jesus Christ is simply beautiful and beautifully simple.

Through His prophets, the Lord has revealed simple truths that will shield us from partaking of poisons that will destroy our souls. The prophet Mormon taught:

> For behold, my brethren, it is given unto you to judge, that ye may know good from evil; and the way to judge is as plain [*simple*], that ye may *know with a perfect knowledge*, as the daylight is from the dark night.
>
> For behold, the Spirit of Christ is given to every man, that he may know good from evil; wherefore, I show unto you the way to judge; for every thing which inviteth to do good, and to persuade to believe in Christ, is sent forth by the power and gift of Christ; wherefore ye may *know with a perfect knowledge* it is of God.
>
> But whatsoever thing persuadeth men to do evil, and believe not in Christ, and deny him, and serve not God, then ye may *know with a perfect knowledge* it is of the devil; for after this manner doth the devil work, for

he persuadeth no man to do good, no, not one; neither do his angels; neither do they who subject themselves unto him. (Moro. 7:15–17, emphasis added)

How simple, how plain, how powerful is this knowledge and this principle. If adhered to, it will keep us securely basking in the Savior's redeeming love and peace.

Sixth, forgive others and be forgiven. It is a fact of life that someone, another imperfect mortal being, will at some point offend or even do harm to us. The mortal in all of us desires to get even, to retaliate, to give back offense for offense. When we come to the knowledge and understanding that *all* sins, transgressions, wrongdoings, and hurtful behavior are an offense before God, we can begin to live one of the most sublime, divine principles attainable by mortal man. God is the lawgiver, not mortal man. We sin against His laws. He, not mortal man, has made the Atonement for mankind—our sins and transgressions. He and He alone has the right and power to forgive men according to His conditions of repentance and in accordance with His divine will. How shocking it is to learn that when we fail to heed His command to forgive all men, we assume the position—hopefully unknowingly and unaware—that we are the lawgiver, we have atoned for the sins of man, and we have the right and power to forgive whom we will forgive based on our own conditions. To maintain the Lord's forgiveness and His peace each day, we must understand and follow His command to forgive all people. The Lord revealed:

And when ye stand praying, forgive, if ye have ought against any: that your Father also which is in heaven may forgive you your trespasses. (Mark 11:25)

My disciples, in days of old, sought occasion against one another and forgave not one another in their hearts; and for this evil they were afflicted and sorely chastened.

Wherefore, I say unto you, that ye ought to forgive one another; for he that forgiveth not his brother his trespasses standeth condemned before the Lord; for there remaineth in him the greater sin.

I, the Lord, will forgive whom I will forgive, but of you it is required to forgive all men. And ye ought to say in your hearts—let God judge between me and thee, and reward thee according to thy deeds. (D&C 64:8–11)

In a session of general conference, Elder Dallin H. Oaks taught and illustrated this celestial principle:

One of the most Godlike expressions of the human soul is the act of forgiveness. Everyone is wronged at some point by someone, and many suffer serious wrongs. Christians everywhere stand in awe of those pioneers who have climbed that steep slope to the spiritual summit attained by those who have heeded the Savior's command to forgive all men (see Matt. 6:14-15; D&C 64:9–10). Forgiveness is mortality's mirror image of the mercy of God *(CR,* Oct. 1989, 81.)

How grateful we are for the knowledge pertaining to the ultimate source of understanding, comfort, and peace. How kind and loving is our Father in heaven. How thankful we are for the atoning sacrifice of Jesus Christ. How merciful He is to invite us to come unto Him by entering through the door of repentance and *receiving* His divine peace to our troubled souls. At peace are those who have come unto Him.

CROWN OF THORNS

FINDING THE REFINER IN THE FURNACE OF AFFLICTION: SEVEN WHO SOUGHT THE SAVIOR

E. DOUGLAS CLARK

THE THREE ISRAELITES IN THE FIERY FURNACE

Speaking to his people through the prophet Isaiah, the Lord declared: "Behold, I have refined thee . . . ; I have chosen thee in the furnace of affliction" (Isa. 48:10). Not long after, the metaphor became a reality for three Israelites—Shadrach, Meshach, and Abed-nego—who refused to worship the colossal golden idol of the Babylonian king, Nebuchadnezzar. When the monarch heard of their refusal, he summoned them and magnanimously offered them another chance.

> Nebuchadnezzar spake and said unto them, Is it true, O Shadrach, Meshach, and Abed-nego, do not ye serve my gods, nor worship the golden image which I have set up?
>
> Now if ye be ready that at what time ye hear the sound of the cornet, flute, harp, sackbut, psaltery, and dulcimer, and all kinds of musick, ye fall down and worship the image which I have made; well: but if ye worship not, ye shall be cast the same hour into the midst of a burning fiery furnace; and who is that God that shall deliver you out of my hands?
>
> Shadrach, Meshach, and Abed-nego, answered and said to the king, O Nebuchadnezzar, we are not careful to answer thee in this matter.

> If it be so, our God whom we serve is able to
> deliver us from the burning fiery furnace, and he will
> deliver us out of thine hand, O king.
>
> But if not, be it known unto thee, O king, that we
> will not serve thy gods, nor worship the golden image
> which thou hast set up. (Dan. 3:14–18)

"Full of fury," Nebuchadnezzar commanded that his "burning fiery furnace" be heated seven times hotter to cleanse his empire from such impudence. He left nothing to chance as he had the three rebels seized by his mightiest soldiers, who themselves perished while casting their prey into the white-hot flames of a certain death.

Eager to see the three rebels burn, the astonished king could not believe what he saw.

> Then Nebuchadnezzar the king . . . rose up in haste,
> and spake, and said unto his counsellors, Did not
> we cast three men bound into the midst of the fire?
> They answered and said unto the king, True, O
> king.
>
> He answered and said, Lo, I see four men loose,
> walking in the midst of the fire, and they have no
> hurt; and the form of the fourth is like the Son of
> God. (Dan. 3:24–25)

Scripture further reports that the three Israelites emerged from the furnace unscathed; not a hair of their heads was singed. The powerful Nebuchadnezzar recognized that he had clashed with a power greater than his own, and hastily decreed torture, death, and destruction of property for anyone speaking anything against the God of Israel. He then promoted the three Israelites within his kingdom.

Nothing further is reported of these three courageous souls, but one might suppose that forever after, they looked back on their entrance into the fiery furnace as the greatest opportunity of their lives, for it was there they met Him described as "like the Son of God."

ADAM LEAVING THE GARDEN

Affliction, adversity, distress; misery, sadness, woe. Whatever word you prefer, such is the common lot of mankind. We come into this world crying, and often leave in anguish. Between these two points of pain our mortal life unfolds, beset too often, it seems, with tribulation that may leave us feeling alone and confused.

But it was not always so. In the Garden of Eden our first parents had no hardships, sickness, or sorrow whatsoever. It was a place of perpetual beauty and ease, all designed for their uninterrupted comfort.

Then, as Genesis relates, everything suddenly changed. Adam bit into the forbidden fruit, plunging his posterity into a world of trouble and turmoil. The very ground itself would be cursed, God told him, and would bring forth "thorns and thistles" to afflict and torment him and his posterity (Gen. 3:18).

In the world's view, the Fall of Adam was the greatest tragedy ever to befall the human race; if only he had refrained from eating the fruit, we would all be living in perfect bliss and without a care in the world, unmarred by the slightest hint of hardship, sickness, pain, or even death. Latter-day Saints know better. The Book of Mormon reveals that if Adam had not partaken, we wouldn't be living at all— at least not in this world. "Adam fell that men might be," explained the ancient prophet Lehi, and then he hastened to add: "and men are, that they might have joy" (2 Ne. 2:25).

Latter-day Saints further know that when Adam ate the famous fruit, he was acting not in disobedience but rather in obedience. The first commandment given to Adam—*and* to Eve—was to "be fruitful, and multiply, and replenish the earth" (Gen. 1:28). Only later came what appears in Genesis to be a second commandment: "But of the tree of the knowledge of good and evil, thou shalt not eat of it" (Gen. 2:17).

But as is evident in our restored scripture, this second commandment was actually more of a warning, for God then added something he has said about no other commandment: "*nevertheless, thou mayest choose for thyself, for it is given to thee;* but remember that I forbid it, for in the day thou eatest thereof thou shalt surely die" (Moses 3:17; emphasis added).

Adam chose to eat and obey the first commandment, thereby opening the door for God's great plan to go forward. In the Book of

Mormon, this plan is referred to as the "plan of happiness" (Alma 42:8, 16). Its presentation to all of us in the premortal life is the reason why we, as the "sons of God" spoken of by Job, once "shouted for joy" (Job 38:7).

Even so, here "in the midst of vexing difficulties," noted Elder Neal A. Maxwell, "sometimes we may wonder . . . what all the shouting was about" (Neal A. Maxwell, *That Ye May Believe* [Salt Lake City: Bookcraft, 1992], 10). We may indeed wonder why the difficulties are so difficult, and why our prior and promised joy seems at times so elusive. Most of all, we may question why we have to undergo affliction, and what purpose, if any, it serves.

Early Christian tradition insists that as Adam was about to leave the garden for a world of affliction, the premortal Savior spoke with him and promised to come to earth in the flesh and endure suffering and crucifixion and death, and then rise again and raise Adam and his posterity in the Resurrection (see "Testament of Adam," translation in James H.Charlesworth, ed., *The Old Testament Pseudepigrapha*, 2 vols. [Garden City, NY: Doubleday, 1983–85], 1:994).

Can it be coincidence that Adam first heard of affliction after choosing obedience, and as he was literally standing face-to-face with Christ, who—as Adam was assured—would mercifully bear the greatest affliction for the benefit of all? Could this setting suggest that each of Adam's posterity, as they live in this world of affliction, must likewise obediently come unto Christ to receive the comfort He alone can give and the eternal life He alone can offer? Might all this even indicate that our afflictions in mortality are divinely designed for our ultimate good with the express purpose of bringing us to Christ and helping us appreciate His atoning affliction for our sake?

If our afflictions reveal our weaknesses and increase our humility; if they intensify our prayers and expand our faith; if they bring us greater repentance and spiritual refinement; if they plant in us a deeper need for the Savior's comfort and strength; if they imbue us with a more profound appreciation of *His* afflictions on our behalf; if they instill in us greater resolve to keep His commandments and follow Him uncon-ditionally; if they increase our empathy for others and our unity with each other and with Him—then surely they have helped us do the very thing on which our eternal salvation depends: come unto Christ.

Only through Christ can we, as Alma would say, feast forever on that "fruit . . . which is most precious, which is sweet above all that is sweet" (Alma 32:42). If the bitterness of our earthly afflictions brings us, as happened with father Adam, to the eternal sweetness offered by Christ, the price we will have paid is small and fleeting. "Sweet," said Shakespeare, "are the uses of adversity" (*As You Like It*, Act 2, scene 1). And sweet is the plan that allowed Adam to eat the fruit in the Garden so that one day he and his posterity could, through their faithfulness, eat the sweet fruit of life eternal.

ABRAHAM ON MOUNT MORIAH

The sweetness offered by the Savior would be bought at a price more bitter than the human mind can comprehend, all out of His unfathomable love. Long after Adam's posterity had rejected that love and had departed from the ways of righteousness, an infant was born into an idolatrous and evil world. His name was Abram, later changed to Abraham, and from the moment he entered this world he was no stranger to affliction.

Rejecting the evil practices of his day, the boy sought truth, and received an opening of the heavens and a restoration of the gospel. Like his descendant Nephi, Abraham talked of Christ, rejoiced in Christ, preached of Christ, and prophesied of Christ. Abraham was even promised that through him and his seed all nations would be blessed to learn of Christ's gospel.

But this promise of posterity went unfulfilled through years and even decades. When Abraham's wife Sarah was past the age of childbearing, angels were sent to this elderly couple to reverse the course of nature. A priesthood blessing brought the miraculous birth of Isaac, whose very name indicates *joy*. Their joy increased further as Isaac grew into a worthy and handsome young man.

When Isaac was about twenty-five, the Savior commanded Abraham: "Take now thy son, thine only son Isaac, whom thou lovest, and get thee into the land of Moriah; and offer him there for a burnt offering upon one of the mountains which I will tell thee of" (Gen. 22:2). Abraham offered no argument, no resistance, no questioning.

Early the next morning Abraham was up chopping the wood for the sacrifice and preparing to leave. Taking Isaac and two servants, and loading up the donkey, Abraham set off on the journey to the land of Moriah. He told no one of the incredible command.

Meanwhile, Abraham wrestled with the fact that the command was absolutely contradictory to all God had promised, to everything Abraham understood and stood for. According to Joseph Smith, it was the hardest thing God could possibly have asked of Abraham.

On the third day of the journey, upon seeing ahead the mountain designated for the sacrifice, Abraham instructed his two servants to remain behind with the donkey. He took the flint and the knife, Isaac took the wood, and together they walked up the mountain. Isaac asked about the lamb for the sacrifice; Abraham replied that God would provide. Reaching the summit, they built the altar and arranged the wood.

Then, according to ancient sources, Abraham revealed to Isaac what God had commanded. Isaac replied that he would be willing to make this sacrifice if his father alone had required it, but knowing that God had commanded it, it was a double honor. But to make sure the sacrifice would go as planned, Isaac asked his father to bind him, lest he lose his nerve at the last moment and spoil the offering.

With Isaac bound face-up on the altar, and with tears streaming down Abraham's face, he bent down and gave his beloved son a final kiss good-bye. Trusting in Christ and in His strength, and trusting still in His promise that Isaac would be the ancestor of prophets and of Christ Himself, Abraham raised the knife to slay his son, when a voice came urgently out of heaven: "Abraham, Abraham!"

The sacrifice was stopped. A ram, discovered in a nearby thicket, was sacrificed in place of Isaac. Abraham was given the unconditional promise of eternal life, and thereby, said Joseph Smith, attained perfect love.

And in the process, Abraham arrived at a new understanding of the Atonement. According to early Christian tradition, as Abraham was about to sacrifice his own son, he foresaw in this act the crucifixion of Christ (see Ernest A. Wallis Budge, ed., *The Book of the Cave of Treasures* [London: The Religious Tract Society], 1927, 150).

If the trial had been necessary to bring Abraham to that perfect love possessed by those who have their calling and election made sure, the trial also taught him—and us—in the most profoundly personal way possible about the depth of love of the Father and the Son in Their offering for all mankind. (See Jacob 4:5; John 3:5; and Ether 12:33.) For that "great and last sacrifice" there would be no ram in the thicket. Thus would all nations be blessed through Jesus the Christ, Son of God, and seed of Abraham.

PAUL IN THE ROMAN EMPIRE

Among Abraham's illustrious descendants was Paul from Tarsus, who first became famous, or infamous, for his zealous persecution of Christians. Only when the resurrected Christ Himself appeared to Paul on the road to Damascus did he abruptly change course and, after a period of preparation, began his new mission as a messenger of Christ.

To preach "of Christ, and Him crucified" (1 Cor. 2:2), Paul traversed great stretches of the Roman Empire at least three times, baptizing, establishing branches of the Church, and strengthening the Saints. Meanwhile, he suffered from what he referred to as "a thorn in the flesh," apparently some sort of painful and chronic ailment which he prayed, unsuccessfully, to have removed (see 2 Cor. 12:7–9).

But this was the least of Paul's troubles, which included all kinds of afflictions, hardships, calamities, beatings, floggings, imprisonments, riots, sleepless nights, and hunger, undergoing numerous difficulties and dangers that brought him often near death (see 2 Cor. 6:4–5; 11:23). As he once recounted,

> Of the Jews five times received I forty stripes save one.
>
> Thrice was I beaten with rods, once was I stoned, thrice I suffered shipwreck, a night and a day I have been in the deep;
>
> In journeyings often, in perils of waters, in perils of robbers, in perils by mine own countrymen . . . in perils in the city, in perils in the wilderness, in perils in the sea, in perils among false brethren;
>
> In weariness and painfulness, in watchings often, in hunger and thirst, in fastings often, in cold and nakedness. (2 Cor. 11:24–27)

Through it all, Paul remained undaunted. "We are troubled on every side, yet not distressed; we are perplexed, but not in despair; Persecuted, but not forsaken; cast down, but not destroyed" (2 Cor. 4:8–9). Paul's perseverance was more than stubbornness: he knew that such suffering was actually necessary for the development of his own Christlike character. "We glory in tribulations . . . knowing that tribulation worketh patience; and patience, experience; and experience, hope" (Rom. 5:3–4). He also saw that such hardship was temporary: "For our light affliction, which is but for a moment, worketh for us a far more exceeding and eternal weight of glory" (2 Cor. 4:17).

Paul understood that the most important of God's gifts was the love of Christ, which became for Paul the supreme reality of his life and the core of his ministry:

> Who shall separate us from the love of Christ? shall tribulation, or distress, or persecution, or famine, or nakedness, or peril, or sword? . . . I am persuaded, that neither death, nor life, nor angels, nor principalities, nor powers, nor things present, nor things to come, nor height, nor depth, nor any other creature, shall be able to separate us from the love of God, which is in Christ Jesus our Lord. (Rom. 8:35, 38–39; see also Rom. 5:5)

Paul's life became a testament to the truth later articulated by Mormon, that "perfect love casteth out all fear" (Moro. 8:16). Paul came to recognize that tribulation was an opportunity for fellowship with Christ, even "the fellowship of his sufferings" (Philip. 3:10).

Through that fellowship, Paul came to know not only his own weakness but also the strength of Christ, who told Paul: "My grace is sufficient for thee: for my strength is made perfect in weakness." Paul understood. "Most gladly therefore will I rather glory in my infirmities, that the power of Christ may rest upon me. Therefore I take pleasure in infirmities, in reproaches, in necessities, in persecutions, in distresses for Christ's sake: for when I am weak, then am I strong" (2 Cor. 12:9–10), and "I can do all things through Christ which strengtheneth me" (Philip. 4:13).

For Paul, the affliction of the present was a small price to pay for the surpassing value of knowing "Christ Jesus my Lord: for whom I have suffered the loss of all things, and do count them but dung, that I may win Christ, and be found in him" (Philip. 3:8–9). For his testimony of Christ, Paul would be executed by command of the Roman Emperor Nero.

It was on the road to Damascus that Paul first met Christ, but it was on numerous other Roman roads of affliction, while traveling to preach of Christ and Him crucified, that Paul became truly acquainted with Him through "the fellowship of his sufferings." It is the same fellowship mentioned by the Nephite prophet Jacob, who hoped that "all men would believe in Christ, and view his death, and *suffer his cross* and bear the shame of the world" (Jacob 1:8; emphasis added) in order to "inherit the kingdom of God" (2 Ne. 9:18).

JOSEPH SMITH IN LIBERTY JAIL

It was the Apostle Paul's example that Joseph Smith remembered when he described the intense persecution that followed the First Vision, persecution that was "often the cause of great sorrow to myself" (JS–H 1:23). And it was Paul, near the end of Joseph's career, whom he again thought of as he reminisced:

> As for the perils which I am called to pass through,
> they seem but a small thing to me, as the envy and
> wrath of man have been my common lot all the days
> of my life; . . . But nevertheless, deep water is what I
> am wont to swim in. It all has become a second
> nature to me; and I feel, like Paul, to glory in tribula-
> tion. . . . (D&C 127:2)

The deepest of those waters had been his four-month imprisonment at Liberty, Missouri, with several of his brethren during the winter of 1838–39 in "the frigid, smelly cellar of a tiny jailhouse, suffering from bad food and poor ventilation" (Richard Lyman Bushman, *Joseph Smith: Rough Stone Rolling* [New York: Alfred A. Knopf], 2005, 373). "Pen, tongue, or angels," Joseph wrote, would be incapable of describing his feelings while there. The low ceiling of the fourteen-foot-square dungeon was not tall enough for him to stand up straight. The rough floor, on which the prisoners slept, was mostly of bare stones, covered here and there with patches of dirty straw. The constant chill of winter seeped through the few scraggly blankets, with the only warmth coming from an occasional fire that spewed forth choking smoke. One visitor described it as a "dark and dismal den, fit only for criminals of the deepest dye" (*Teachings of the Presidents of the Church: Joseph Smith*, 360).

The coarse food was "so filthy that [they] could not eat it until [they] were driven to it" (*TPCJS*, 360), and repeatedly contained poison that caused the prisoners days of vomiting and delirium. Joseph described the jail as a "hell, surrounded with demons . . . where we are compelled to hear nothing but blasphemous oaths, and witness a scene of blasphemy, and drunkenness and hypocrisy, and debaucheries of every description" (*HC*, 3:290).

But it was more than his own affliction that weighed heavily on the Prophet: it was also the terrible sufferings of his people outside the prison, the Latter-day Saints whom he loved and led and longed to protect, but was powerless to help as they were being mobbed, robbed, violently abused, and killed. It was a dagger to the heart of the deeply compassionate Prophet, compounding his own personal tribulation.

About a month into the imprisonment, Joseph and his counselors wrote a letter to the Saints echoing several New Testament passages. The words breathed courage and encouragement, and spoke of purpose in suffering:

> Neither think [it] strange concerning the fi[e]ry trials with which we are tried as though some strange thing had happened unto us. Remember that all have been partakers of like afflictions. Therefore rejoice in our afflictions by which we are perfected and through which the captain of our salvation was perfected also. (Bushman, 373)

But as the months wore on, the prisoners wore down. "Our souls have been bowed down," wrote the Prophet, and "my nerve trembles from long confinement" (Elder Jeffrey R. Holland, "Lessons from

Liberty Jail," in *BYU Magazine,* 63:1 [Winter 2009], 35). And as Elder Holland pointed out, Joseph was not in prison for anything that he had done wrong, but precisely because he had done right. In that unrelenting and prolonged hell, with no respite for the Prophet or his people outside the prison, he wrote them a lengthy letter in which he began by echoing language of the imprisoned Apostle Paul (see Phil. 1:1): "Your humble servant, Joseph Smith, Jun., prisoner for the Lord Jesus Christ's sake . . ." (*HC* 3:289–290).

As he continued and recounted some of the horrible persecution, his suffering soul spontaneously cried out in agony to the God who seemed so far away:

> O God, where art thou? And where is the pavilion that covereth thy hiding place? How long shall thy hand be stayed, and thine eye, yea thy pure eye, behold from the eternal heavens the wrongs of thy people and of thy servants, and thine ear be penetrated with their cries? Yea, O Lord, how long shall they suffer these wrongs and unlawful oppressions, before thine heart shall be softened toward them, and thy bowels be moved with compassion toward them? O Lord God Almighty . . . stretch forth thy hand. . . . (D&C 121:1–4)

There was no immediate answer. What did arrive was a packet of letters, one from his beloved Emma, striking a tender chord in Joseph's heart and bringing him to tears—and to the point, as he described, that "all enmity, malice and hatred, and past differences, misunderstandings and mismanagements are slain victorious at the feet of hope." What followed was one of the greatest revelations ever given on the powers and blessings of the priesthood:

> And when the heart is sufficiently contrite, then the voice of inspiration steals along and whispers, My son, peace be unto thy soul; thine adversity and thine afflictions shall be but a small moment; and then if thou endure it well, God shall exalt thee on high; thou shalt triumph over all thy foes . . . (*HC* 3:293–294, including D&C 121:7–8)

Additional words of comfort and consolation followed, and finally, the greatest lesson, the greatest insight of all. Referring to the terrible things that had happened and could yet happen to His valiant Prophet, the Savior gently explained: "The Son of Man hath descended below them all" (D&C 122:8).

Thus also did Joseph discover, there amidst the squalor and the suffering, the very presence of the Savior. As B. H. Roberts recounted, "Joseph Smith sought God in this rude prison, and found him" (*HC* 1:526). But where was God when Joseph had cried out in agony for Him? Years earlier a revelation had told Joseph that he would have many afflictions. "But endure them," the Savior instructed, and then promised: "for, lo, *I am with thee, even unto the end of thy days*" (D&C 24:8; emphasis added). The Savior had been in the wretched dungeon with His valiant Prophet all along, intentionally hidden from his view to allow him to experience a tiny taste of the bitter loneliness endured by the Savior when He had suffered for Joseph and all of mankind.

TRANSFORMATION IN THE FURNACE OF AFFLICTION

In all ages of the world, as followers of Christ have found themselves in the furnace of affliction, they have made the discovery of their lives: it is there where they encounter Him who was once "afflicted" and "wounded for our transgressions" (Isa. 53:4–5); Him who "suffere[d] the pains of all men, yea, the pains of every living creature, both men, women, and children, who belong to the family of Adam" (2 Ne. 9:21); Him from whom "blood [came] from every pore, so great [was] his anguish for the wickedness and the abominations of his people" (Mosiah 3:7); Him who took upon Himself our "infirmities, that his bowels may be filled with mercy" (Alma 7:12). It is He who sits, as described by the prophet Malachi, "as a refiner and purifier of silver" (Mal. 3:3) to purify His people.

The story is told of a woman who, having read that verse in Malachi, visited a silversmith to learn about the process of refining silver. She watched as he carefully held a piece of silver over the hottest part of the fire to burn away the impurities.

Curious, the woman asked if he had to remain by the fire for the entire process. Yes, the man replied, because if the silver were left for a moment too long it would be consumed.

Thanking him, the woman began to leave and then suddenly turned back to ask a final question. "How do you know when the silver is fully refined?"

"When I see my image in it," came the reply.

Mormon's great hope was that when the Savior would finally appear in glory, "we shall be like him, for we shall see him as he is; that we may have this hope; that we may be purified even as he is pure" (Moro. 7:48).

If such transformation requires our entrance into a furnace of affliction, it may well prove our greatest opportunity to there meet our Refiner and Redeemer, who waits to lovingly welcome us and prepare us for eternal joy with Him.

JOY OF THE LORD

THERE NEVER WAS A HAPPIER TIME

TODD B. PARKER

Even though today's tumultuous times have been foreseen and fore-told, questions inevitably arise as we personally witness them from the front-row seats of the latter days. Why does the Lord allow the inno-cent to suffer? Why do the righteous often die and the wicked go free? Why aren't the innocent protected? If the Lord loves His children, how can He permit them to be treated so horribly? The Book of Mormon provides a perspective that explains how "even these things . . . mani-fest a loving Father in Heaven" (Boyd K. Packer, "The Play and the Plan," CES satellite broadcast, 7 May 1995).

WHY THE BOOK OF MORMON?
Hope in Christ
The Book of Mormon contains 6,607 verses, 3,925 of which refer to Christ. In fact, some form of His name is mentioned every 1.7 verses (see Susan Easton Black, "Names of Christ in the Book of Mormon," *Ensign,* July 1978, 60–61). Herein lies a key as to why the Book of Mormon is a handbook for these turbulent times in which we live—it repeatedly teaches that Christ is the unshakeable foundation of our hope.

The prophet Mormon wrote a letter to his son Moroni concerning the hope he had in spite of all the wickedness and sorrow he had seen, and the foundation upon which it was based: "And what is it that ye shall hope for? Behold I say unto you that ye shall have hope through the atonement of Christ and the power of his resurrection, to be raised unto life eternal, and this because of your faith in him according to the promise" (Moro. 7:41).

Thus, our hope is to be based on Christ and His Atonement, and our faith centered in His promise that we may be raised up to eternal life. In a day so often filled with great despair, this hope in Christ is what makes this record such a powerful source of peace.

In his farewell address, King Benjamin also taught his people that their hope must be centered in Christ. He taught that Jesus of Nazareth is the only true hope we have for salvation. Without hope in the true and living Christ, our expectation of better things to come falls into the realm of wishful thinking: "And moreover, I say unto you, that there shall be no other name given nor any other way nor means whereby salvation can come unto the children of men, only in and through the name of Christ, the Lord Omnipotent" (Mosiah 3:17).

Hope in Christ is the very essence of the plan of salvation. The entire plan of happiness is founded in, predicated upon, and accomplished by the Atonement of Christ.

FINDING HOPE IN ADVERSITY
Adversity as Part of the Plan of Happiness
In the Book of Mormon we read, "Behold there never was a happier time among the people of Nephi" (Alma 50:23). When I ask students to what time that scripture refers, their answers vary: "When Jesus was ministering to the Nephites?" or "During the time of Fourth Nephi?" or "When Lehi arrived in the promised land?"

Students are often shocked to discover that Mormon used this verse to describe the Nephites' disposition in a time of war. Although it was a period of great calamity and destruction, the Nephites did not allow their grim circumstances to determine their happiness. In fact, not only was their current adversity not affecting their joy—it may have even been adding to it.

How could that be?

Shortly before his death, the prophet Lehi blessed each of his children. Lehi's final blessing to his son Jacob contains a basic key to understanding adversity and trial. Trials are actually a vital part of the plan of happiness. Without trials and adversity, true happiness would not be available to us. The plan of happiness called for our first parents to fall from a paradisaical state of "no joy, for they knew no misery" (2 Ne. 2:23) to a telestial state wherein "they might have joy" (2 Ne. 2:25). Following the Fall, Adam acknowledged that "because of my transgression my eyes are opened and in this life I shall have joy" (Moses 5:10).

A sense of why we come to earth, why God gives us commandments, and why we are tried is explained by Alma: "God had appointed that these things [living in a fallen condition] should come unto man . . . therefore . . . [He] . . . made known unto them the plan of redemption, which had been prepared from the foundation of the world. . . . Therefore God gave unto them commandments, after having made known unto them the plan of redemption" (Alma 12:28–32).

Happiness and joy are not gifts that arrive in a package or that are enjoyed in a vacuum. They may only be experienced in concert with opposites. We must experience pain to appreciate well-being, difficulties to develop courage, and death to understand eternal life. Muscles need opposition to gain strength. Faith must confront doubt to grow. Adversity is an integral variable for progression in the equation of life.

That adversity is necessary for growth, and that happiness and joy are the outcomes of experience and trials was known by all of us in the premortal existence. Elder Spencer W. Kimball observed:

> We knew before we were born that we were coming to the earth for bodies and experience and that we would have joys and sorrows, ease and pain, comforts and hardships, health and sickness, successes and disappointments, and we knew also that after a period of life we would die. We accepted all these eventualities with a glad heart, eager to accept both the favorable and unfavorable. We eagerly accepted the chance to come earthward even though it might be for only a day or a year. Perhaps we were not so much concerned whether we should die of disease, of accident, or of senility. We were willing to take life as it came and as we might organize and control it, and this without murmur, complaint, or unreasonable demands. (*Faith*

Precedes the Miracle [Salt Lake City, Utah: Deseret Book Company], 1976, 106)

Brigham Young attributed Joseph Smith's greatness to the trials he endured. "Joseph could not have been perfected, though he had lived a thousand years, if he had received no persecution. If he had lived a thousand years, and led this people, and preached the gospel without persecution, he would not have been perfected as well as he was at the age of thirty-nine years" (see *Journal of Discourses* 2:7).

If happiness is predicated upon righteousness, and righteousness is predicated upon opposites, then happiness and righteousness must involve adversity. Hence, it must be accepted that adversity plays a role in acquiring happiness.

CHRIST IS OUR DELIVERER FROM ALL TYPES OF ADVERSITY

In the very first chapter of the Book of Mormon, the prophet Nephi stated his purpose for keeping this record: "But behold, I, Nephi, will show unto you that the tender mercies of the Lord are over all those whom he hath chosen, because of their faith, to make them mighty even unto the power of deliverance" (1 Ne. 1:20).

Nephi states his objective in the first few lines of his record—to show the reader how merciful the Lord is to all who will allow Him to be their deliverer. As explained earlier, adversity, trials, and hardships are all part of the plan of happiness. However, all trials and adversities are not cut from the same cloth. Under certain circumstances, our choices help determine the type of adversity we may experience. Following the death of his wife, Elder Richard G. Scott spoke of the role of trials and that they come to us through two different avenues:

> No one wants adversity. Trials, disappointments, sadness, and heartache come to us from two basically different sources. Those who transgress the laws of God will always have those challenges. The other reason for adversity is to accomplish the Lord's own purposes in our life that we may receive the refinement that comes from testing. It is vitally important for each of us to identify that from these two sources

come our trials and challenges, for the corrective action is very different. *(CR,* Oct. 1995, 18)

There are two valuable lessons we can learn from this. First of all, we can avoid many of the trials that the world will face in these latter days simply by making righteous choices. And yet even when our unwise choices bring crushing adversity upon us, the Lord has promised that if we repent He will be there to deliver us.

The second principle we learn is that there will also be adversity that comes to us even though we are living righteous lives. Yes, "bad things" do happen to "good people"—if only to make them better. Again here, if we put our trust in the Lord, He has promised that He will deliver us. And yet it should be remembered that His deliverance may not come by removing our trials, but in helping us to bear them.

As we seek to find hope in the trials and adversity that these latter days will surely bring—whether induced by us or allowed by the Lord—let us look to Christ as our Deliverer.

FINDING HOPE IN TRAGEDY
How is it that tragedy fits into the plan of happiness? Wouldn't temptations and trials alone meet the requirements of the plan?

After abridging the section of the large plates that recounted the major Nephite/Lamanite wars (see Alma 42–62) and then abridging a major portion of the account of the Gadianton band (see Hel. 1–11), Mormon paused to reflect and recount some lessons that the readers of the last days should have indelibly impressed upon their minds. As we latter-day readers come to phrases such as, "and thus we can behold" or "and we may see," we should realize that Mormon is doing more than just adding a commentary to the record. He is petitioning us to learn pertinent lessons from the mistakes of past civilizations so we can avoid repeating them.

As Mormon appeals to the latter-day readers of his record, he writes:

> And thus we can behold how false, and also the unsteadiness of the hearts of the children of men; yea, we can see that the Lord in his great infinite goodness

doth bless and prosper those who put their trust in him.

Yea, and we may see at the very time when he doth prosper his people, yea, in the increase of their fields, their flocks and their herds, and in gold, and in silver, and in all manner of precious things of every kind and art; sparing their lives, . . . and in fine, doing all things for the welfare and happiness of his people; yea, then is the time that they do harden their hearts, and do forget the Lord their God, and do trample under their feet the Holy One—yea, and this because of their ease, and their exceedingly great prosperity.

And thus we see that except the Lord doth chasten his people with many afflictions, yea, except he doth visit them with death and with terror, and with famine and with all manner of pestilence, they will not remember him. (Hel. 12:1–3; emphasis added)

Mormon lamented that as soon as the Lord blesses His people with peace, prosperity, riches, and happiness, that is exactly the time they begin to forget Him. Such was the effect of the 9/11 tragedy on Americans.

In a Church Education System satellite broadcast delivered on May 7, 1995, Elder Packer singled out the word *terror* as used by Mormon in Helaman 12:3. He explained that a careful examination of those verses would help members understand the role of terrorism and tragedy in the plan of salvation. Is it possible that as a people of the United States, we had prospered in our fields, flocks, gold, silver, and art (to use Mormon's words) to the point that we had forgotten "the Lord [our] God" and trampled under our feet the "Holy One" because of our "ease and exceedingly great prosperity" (Hel. 12:3)? Did the Lord allow us to be chastened with "affliction," with "death," and with "terror" so we would remember Him? Some changes in our nation following the terrorist attack tend to validate Mormon's message.

On the Sunday following the attack, athletic arenas were filled with humble, tearful people—praying, singing, and waving flags.

That same week many churches that had previously been filled with empty pews were filled to capacity. The buying of hot dogs, beer, and peanuts at ball parks was replaced with the partaking of the emblems of the Lord's last supper at churches. The screaming, chanting, and self-indulging in football stadiums was replaced with meditation, reflection, and a desire to commune with God in sacred places.

Is it possible that the "God of this land" on the Sunday following September 11 shifted from the "worship" of athletics to the worship of Jesus Christ? The week before the attack, Congress was filled with bipartisan bickering. The week following the attack, both houses of Congress stood united on the steps of the Capitol and sang "God Bless America."

There was also a shift in topics on radio and television. Prior to the attack, political correctness prevented talk show hosts, reporters, or news personalities from mentioning God, prayer, or faith publicly. After the attack, these terms became commonplace. Previous voices against the military, prayer in school, and displays of faith fell silent. The group who had booed the Boy Scouts during the flag ceremony of a political convention (because of the Boy Scouts of America's stand against homosexuality) stood with hands over their hearts during later flag ceremonies as the fallen were remembered. A record-setting number of standing ovations was given to a United States president in a joint session of Congress as he addressed the nation using the terms "God," "faith," "prayer," and "grace." Callers to talk show hosts, who earlier complained about the government, were suddenly found waving flags and defending freedom.

What changed? Perhaps the tragic events of September 11 caused the people of a choice land to start acting like a choice people—instead of a people who complain about choices.

In an attempt to call his people to repentance, Alma gave up his judgment seat to Nephihah to provide himself a better circumstance to "preach the word of God" to "stir [the Nephites] up in remembrance of their duty" (Alma 4:20). As a part of his discourse to the inhabitants of Zarahemla, Alma said: "The good shepherd doth call after you; and if you will hearken unto his voice he will bring you into his fold, and ye are his sheep" (Alma 5:60). During the Savior's ministry in Jerusalem, He referred to Himself as a shepherd using the words, "I am the good shepherd, and know my sheep, and am known of mine. As the Father knoweth me, even so know I the Father: and I lay down my life for the sheep" (John 10:14–15).

Many people in the Western hemisphere may not understand Jesus' imagery of shepherds and sheep since they are more familiar with sheepherders than shepherds. Western sheepherders often use dogs or ride horses to drive large numbers of sheep to desired locations. In the Middle East, it is done differently. Shepherds often have small flocks, and their sheep are more like pets. They have names for each sheep or lamb similar to the way Westerners have names for pet dogs or cats.

Once, while I was touring in Israel, our group watched a shepherd with his sheep. The shepherd led his sheep. He walked in front and the sheep followed behind. The sheep for the most part followed the shepherd in single file. When the shepherd came to a busy road, he first crossed the road himself. He then called each sheep by name to cross the road one by one as traffic permitted. The sheep knew his voice. They responded to that voice in obedience for their own safety. That good shepherd knew his sheep. He loved them. He protected them. The sheep trusted the shepherd with their lives.

On another occasion, a Church Education System group touring the Holy Land came upon a shepherd carrying a small lamb in a large pocket inside his garment. A member of the group noted a splint on the lamb's leg. When asked how the leg had become wounded, the shepherd replied, "I broke it." The shepherd then explained that the little lamb had kept wandering away from the flock, putting his life in jeopardy. This good shepherd had broken the lamb's leg so the lamb would have to be carried. Of necessity, the lamb would learn to depend on the shepherd and consequently remain free from the physical dangers that seemed to entice him (see George Horton, "Insights from the Holy Land," CES Old Testament Symposium, 1991).

In a similar fashion, Christ, the Good Shepherd, allows us—His sheep—to experience trials, adversity, and "spiritual broken legs" to teach us dependence on Him. If we, as His sheep, through this process of adversity, learn to stay close to Him and let Him carry us, we can then truly be a part of His fold and He becomes our Shepherd.

If we choose, these last days may be to us as the broken leg was to the lamb, drawing us closer to Him. The Good Shepherd knows His sheep and provides them not only with hope, but also with protection in His fold and kingdom—whether we are gently led there, or humbled and carried. May we see the wisdom of His plan and may it bring to us "hope through the atonement of Christ . . . to be raised unto eternal life . . . because of [our] faith in him . . ." (Moro. 7:41).

KING OF KINGS

TRUSTING THE LORD

JOY SAUNDERS LUNDBERG

The following three personal experiences have given me immense comfort and peace, and laid a foundation in carrying me through other trials that have come along.

1. As a child: I remember a conversation with my father a long time ago when I was just twelve years old. He had been reading the scriptures to our family regarding the last days. The calamities seemed overwhelming to me and I was more than a little scared by the terrible prospect of such a frightening future. Looking for comfort I said, "But, Daddy, what will happen to me if I'm on the earth when it happens?" He put his arm around me and said, "Oh, sweetheart, you don't need to be afraid. All you need to do is keep the commandments, and the Lord will be with you. If you die, then you will be ready and He will receive you with open arms. If you live, then He will walk beside you and help you through whatever lies ahead. So either way, you'll be just fine, as long as you are doing your best to keep His commandments."

I can remember deciding at that moment that I would do my very best to keep the commandments, and a feeling of peace filled my whole being. That teaching of my father has given me guidance and comfort throughout my life.

2. As a young mother: Another incident occurred when our first three children were very young. At that time I had been diagnosed with a serious illness. My husband was a pilot in the U.S. Air Force, and we were a long way from home. My Grandma Saunders came to

visit us and taught me an important concept about prayer. She said, "I know you have prayed about your illness. And you have had a priesthood blessing. Now here's what I want to know: After you say your prayers and lay your burdens at the Lord's feet as He tells us to do, do you say 'amen' and then pick them up again? Or do you trust Him enough to leave them for Him to carry as He promised He would?"

Her words sunk deep into my heart, and I followed her wise counsel. The blessing came, and I was healed. Not all blessings in my life have been answered so directly, but the principle remains strongly in force in my life.

3. As a mother of grown children: We have five children and some have faced difficult challenges, including one daughter who is mentally disabled. I remember well a time several years ago when my husband and I were concerned over difficulties our three eldest children were having. One had lost his job, one was having marital problems, and our disabled child was having serious, ongoing challenges. It all seemed so overwhelming to me. Burdened with worry I arose early in the morning to do my personal scripture study, preceded by prayer. On this particular morning I prayed with all my heart for the individual needs of these three children. I cried fervently to the Lord in their behalf. I was experiencing the full dimensions of a heavy heart. It was literally painful.

After the prayer, I picked up my Book of Mormon and began reading where I had left off the previous morning, in 2 Nephi, chapter 9. When I read the third verse, I knew from the peace that filled my whole being that the Lord had just answered my prayers through this scripture. I read it over and over, "I speak unto you these things that ye may rejoice, and lift up your heads forever, because of the blessings which the Lord God shall bestow upon your children."

I didn't need to worry any more. I just needed to pray and trust in the Lord. He would help our children. And He did. It took time, but each one has been blessed with the very things he or she needed.

From these experiences I learned to "Trust in the Lord with all thine heart; and lean not unto thine own understanding. In all thy ways acknowledge him, and he shall direct thy paths" (Prov. 3:5–6). This principle of trusting the Lord has seen me and my family through many troubled times. There is great comfort in knowing that we can trust the Lord, and He will look out for us and direct us. All we need to do is acknowledge Him and trust Him as we work toward solutions to our problems.

It doesn't seem to matter what our troubles are—sickness, loss of a job, a troubled economy, a wayward child, or any number of difficulties—we simply need to hold on to our faith and trust in the Lord. The ancient prophet Micah faced his own problems and, in so doing, gave us a pattern. He said, "when I sit in darkness, the Lord shall be a light unto me" (Micah 7:8). In order to see the light during dark times in our lives, we must allow the light to come in, even invite it in through our faith and prayers. In so doing we may see opportunities that we had never before considered. Answers eventually come when we trust in the Lord and receive His light.

President Gordon B. Hinckley was a master at inviting in the light and having faith. Many times we heard him say the words, "Don't get discouraged. Things will work out." As we look back on our life, sure enough, most things have worked out; and for those that haven't yet worked out, we must trust that they will.

None of us knows what lies ahead, but one thing is certain; we don't need to worry about it. We just need to "trust in the Lord."

OF SUCH IS THE KINGDOM OF GOD

A SINGLE
FALLEN SPARROW

TONI SORENSON

There is a sparrow outside my hotel window, hopping and chirping like it might be lost. I cannot rescue it because a great wall of glass separates us. All I can do is watch the tiny creature, say a simple prayer, and feel pity for its frailty.

I am on a sort of pilgrimage, a journey to the land where Jesus' lungs first filled with air, where He cried and laughed and learned to walk just like every human baby . . . by trying, stumbling, falling, and rising again. The ground here is hard and rocky, and I wonder at how many times Mary must have kissed scraped knees and bruised elbows. I can almost hear Joseph cheering on his determined little boy as a beaming Jesus learned to balance Himself along uneven paths of stone.

This is the Holy Land, where the Son of God became the Son of Man.

Yesterday, an aged priest cloaked in black robes looked at me with eyes gone milky. His gnarled fingers patted my hand. "You've come to find comfort in the Christ?"

His question made me stop and think. "Of course," I told him.

"You will not find Jesus in the tomb. He is not there."

I nodded.

The priest smiled. "It seems a bit foolish, doesn't it, that people travel far and come in throngs just to peek inside to be sure that it is still empty?"

Silly, and yet comforting, I thought.

"Jesus cannot be found in a place," he said before turning to the next pilgrim.

The sparrow turns my attention back to the present. The bird is so small, so frantic. A head not much bigger than my thumb bobs up and down as the bird pecks at dry stones. Its wings are tucked tight against its little body, and I assess that something must be broken. Otherwise, wouldn't it just fly off the ledge to freedom?

Beyond the sparrow, the Mount of Olives rises in layers. All around me Jerusalem yawns and stretches in the morning light. Its hues are the same muted whites and tans and browns of the sparrow. In this setting, such a bird is designed to blend with its surroundings. God, the Great Creator, the Architect of Life, planned it that way. In His infinite mercy, He made it so the sparrow could find shelter and reprieve, because the other birds of Israel are bigger, stronger, more aggressive. The first day I arrived here I saw a hawk dive after a sparrow in flight. God is mindful of small sparrows.

Poor sparrow, I think. It has me worried. It is now thudding its little brown breast against the glass. He seems to look right at me, his chirp crying, "Help me, please."

"I would if I could, but I cannot reach you. The window is sealed, and the ledge has no access."

Who is being silly now? I'm talking to a sparrow.

I pray again, and gently yet profoundly, the Lord reminds me that no so long ago, I was that fallen bird.

Alone. Afraid. Broken. Battered. I'd lost my way and my hope. I'd fallen from the high place that had been my sanctuary. When I crashed, it felt like everything inside of me shattered.

For a season of despair I laid there motionless. Utterly defeated. Out of hope. In my own eyes I was a worthless, fallen sparrow. But God's eye was on me. Eventually He came to bind my broken wings, to hold me in His unfailing arms, to nourish my starving spirit until I was strong enough to flutter my wings, lift my head high, to chirp a song, and finally to soar. I was able to "achieve liftoff" because the atoning power of Christ's gift always, always lifts us upward. It covers all of mortality's feelings and experiences. It redeems and restores those who have tumbled, those who lay torn and dying, those who are discarded and forsaken by everyone except the One who will never forsake His own children. I found that it doesn't matter if we were shot down out of flight by enemy fire or if our own charted course led us head-on into a wall. The Savior doesn't ask, "Why are you there?" he simply waits for us to chirp out the faintest call for help so that He can rush to rescue us.

I'm still not wholly healed. There are parts of me that I realize are raw, parts that bleed unexpectedly at an unkind word or accusation. Memories are sharp and can slice an old wound new. I have to do as Paul admonished . . . "bringing into captivity every thought to the obedience of Christ . . ." (2 Cor. 10:5). I have to be careful what I think, not believe all that people say—or even what I tell myself—but find out what Jesus has to say on the matter and believe Him.

With God's help I've come a long way, and I look at that bird and give thanks. Then as if on cue, a little breeze stirs, and that single sparrow chirps again, stretches out his tattered wings, points his beak skyward, and is lifted from the ground up into the air.

As I watch that little marvel of design take flight I realize that yes, I am in the Holy Land to seek comfort of the Christ. It's where I find it and what that discovery teaches me that leaves me in awe.

It is in the take-off of a fallen sparrow. In the beat of my own grateful heart. In the query of a priest who has devoted his life to bringing to others the comfort of Christ.

The priest was right, and hard as I try, I don't find my Savior in a place—not in a tomb, not in a shrine, not even in a church. I find him on the faces of the people, especially the children. Comfort comes most powerfully when I interact with those people, especially the children.

Come; relive my journey as we walk down a narrow Jerusalem street. It's early, early morning, the sky is yellow with the promise of the rising sun, and the air is filled with birdsong and honking horns. There is no beep-beeping here. In Jerusalem, a driver lays on the horn until the driver behind him does the same and so on and so on until the whole street is honking in unison. Voices rise around me speaking Hebrew, Arabic, English, Spanish, Japanese, and many other dialects I can't identify. Maybe because Babel was located only a few borders away. In spite of all the chaos, there is the sound of the laughter of school children; in spite of the pungency of grilling meat and burning car fuel, there is a faint fragrance of blooming spring flowers.

On my journey I find Jesus as I stop to give a blind man a few shekels. I cannot restore his sight, but as I look into empty sockets where eyes should be, I know without doubt that Jesus healed the blind.

I see the ravages of leprosy on both women and men . . . their skin is scarred and marked and I think how Jesus healed them, too. Not just from the physical pain and suffering, but from the shame and embarrassment of feeling ugly and unwanted by society.

I kiss a Jewish grandmother's cheek as she holds out a fistful of basil for me to buy. As my lips are pressed to her warm, leathered cheek, she whispers in Hebrew, "Toda." *Thank you.* How many times did Jesus hear those very words? Though He would most likely have spoken Aramaic, He would have understood "Toda," and He would have appreciated.

I think of how humble Jesus was as He set the example of gratitude "I thank thee, O Father . . ." (Matt. 11:25).

My feet meander along the banks of the Jordan River, and I am humbled as throngs of believers rent white baptismal uniforms and are immersed in the name of the Father, the Son, and the Holy Ghost. They pay for this privilege in shekels. The river, I think, must be filthy with the sins of so many . . . but then I realize that our sins don't wash down the Jordan River or a baptismal font in a church . . . they are carried upon the shoulders of the Savior of the world—"he bare the sin of many, and made intercession for the transgressors" (Isa. 53:12).

I feel such sadness. Indiscernible sorrow. I'm so sorry for the weight the Savior bore to carry my sins. I cannot seem to shed the heaviness of this holy journey. For days and days and days I feel such heaviness as I move from site to site, as I join the masses and trek the route that Jesus is said to have taken between His condemnation by Pilate and His crucifixion and burial—the Via Dolorosa. For many Christian pilgrims it is a highlight, a meaningful experience. For me it is torture.

What is wrong with me? Why can't I feel the rapture and the passion? What is amiss in me that makes me want to run away from the places marked most holy?

Father, teach me, I pray, *of Thy Son.* I ache to know Him better. I need the comfort of the Christ because I realize that this broken sparrow is not as strong and healed as she thought she was. *Open my heart, open my eyes, my mind to the life of Thy Son . . . that I might know Him better. That I might feel His comfort.*

I take refuge in the Garden Tomb, a place where finally I can breathe. I'm seated on a stone bench with my back pressed to a wall when the Master Teacher decides the time has come to teach this pupil a lesson not to be forgotten.

The garden is beautiful. Peaceful. Here, sunlight filters through budding leaves and neatly pruned branches. Here, the weight begins to lift. I've been to the tomb. I've witnessed for myself that it is empty. Jesus has risen. All along the way I've tried to look for sparrows, signs of God's tender mercies to His children. This day in this place I see no sparrows. What I see are tourists filing through in search of the same thing that I seek . . . a closer walk with Thee. A group of at least a hundred beautiful black faces beam . . . all the way from Nigeria. Another group is from Korea. A man has brought his family all the way from Finland, so that his children might go back and testify that the tomb could not hold the Christ.

I'm looking straight down a rock pathway where a beam of pure, white sunlight dances. I'm fixated on that spot when I imagine I see Jesus as a young boy . . . barreling around that corner. His sandaled foot slides on the mossy path and He almost falls, but He catches Himself and laughs at His near mishap. He darts away, but the sound of absolute joy reverberates through the echo of His laughter.

Then comes a kind of comfort that I have never experienced. A peace that passeth understanding. A spectacular joy in knowing that Jesus didn't just die for us. His life was not just about sorrow, pain, and suffering. It wasn't even all about atoning. "I am come that they might have life, and that they might have it more abundantly" (John 10:10).

It is as if Jesus is giving me permission to forgive myself for all that He has already pardoned me for. That He is extending to me an invitation to live. Not to merely exist, but to truly live and have a marvelous time doing it!

The gospel of Jesus is about joy. It is good news and glad tidings. "Adam fell that men might be; and men are, that they might have joy"

(2 Ne. 2:25). God has a plan in place, and even if enemy fire takes us down while we are soaring, God WANTS to lift us. He WANTS us to be happy. To know love and peace and plenty. He WANTS to rescue us from our foes and from ourselves.

What I was being taught in those defining moments gave new meaning to His bid, "Come, follow me."

Elder Neal A. Maxwell made it clear: "God is very serious about the joy of his children!" ("Called to Serve," fireside address given at Brigham Young University, Mar. 27, 1994).

If I were to follow Jesus, I had some serious attitude adjustments to make, some hard choices, many, many more lessons to learn about life. He asks us to learn of Him (see Matt. 11:29). I'd learned that He was powerful, humble, grateful, perfectly obedient. I'd learned that He defined love, that He was ultimately victorious over death.

What I had yet to learn and what I am still learning is found between the lines of scriptures—but it is there for those who will see it. He didn't just love us . . . He loved life. He loved His Father. His earthly family. He loved Himself. All in a healthy, perfectly balanced way. Jesus lived every moment; He allowed Himself the highs and lows, the tears and the laughter. He embraced all that came his way as experience . . . life's most effective teacher.

Jesus was born a baby, innocent and helpless. He "increased in wisdom and stature, and in favour with God and man" (Luke 2:52). To *increase in wisdom* means He had to learn along the way. Imagine the joy He found in lacing His own shoes for the first time. In learning to count. In reciting the passages from the Torah. Try to picture His hands taking a blade and carving the figure of a single sparrow out of olive wood, then beaming as He showed it to Joseph, His mortal father, for approval.

Jesus knew the satisfaction of hard work. His nails wore dirt. His muscles ached and His skin baked. He planted, He cultivated, He harvested. He was part of a family. Families worked side by side. He was part of a community who also worked and worshiped together.

Mary and Joseph were the parents of other children. Of course Jesus helped to tend and care for His siblings. Of course they wandered the steep incline of their village, exploring all of nature's wonders. Of course Jesus tasted olives right from the tree. Of course He smelled the rich aroma of His mother's baking bread.

He loved music and still does. I imagine Mary was like other Jewish mothers who sang the scriptures to their children. No wonder, then, that the Lord said, "For my soul delighteth in the song of the heart; yea, the song of the righteous is a prayer unto me, and it shall be answered with a blessing upon their heads" (D&C 25:12).

The scriptures were never a chore, but a blessing to be read and learned and lived. Obedience was a privilege. The cadence of life's balance could be found in the rhythm of the scriptures read aloud and lived even louder.

He learned the miracle of His own body—how to strengthen it, challenge it, care for it in all ways. It's all there in the scriptures . . . when Jesus was hungry He ate; when He was weary, He slept. He knew the joy of putting His head into the welcoming softness of a pillow.

Of course He could name all the different birds and animals and fishes; the plants and trees that He Himself had first placed here to grow and multiply and replenish.

How He must have marveled as the Spirit taught Him His true identity.

I've splashed in the waters of Galilee. I've breathed in the scent that happens when earth meets water. My heart has danced at the beauty of seeing a rainbow arc over the sea of Christ's fishermen. Imagine what Jesus felt as He counted the colors in a rainbow, hues He'd chosen from His own artist's palette.

Jesus lived that we might live! I suspect that there was a sense of adventure in Him as He made the arduous pilgrimages from Nazareth into the Holy City. That His eyes took in new sights, that His mind took in new truths. It took courage for a young boy to teach the rabbis at the temple. Jesus never lacked for courage.

It took patience to wait until His time to teach was come. What did He do in the meantime? He grew. He learned. He lived. He made friends. He fostered relationships. No chance to better Himself was sacrificed to idleness.

When news of this man Jesus, His passion and His life, reached Nathanael, the question was posed, "Can there any good thing come out of Nazareth?" (John 1:46). Philip, knowing Jesus, had to smile at that question. "Come and see," was his reply.

Come and see for yourself. See with your spiritual eyes what the Spirit has to teach you about how Christ lived and how He wants you and me to live.

With obedience. With zeal. No more mediocre Mormons. No more wimpy, whining children. God wants us to become like Him. We can't do that by staying back, staying down, or staying put. We have to experience what it means to follow Jesus . . . in obedience, in love, in complete surrender.

In order for Jesus to fully understand what it feels to be a fallen bird, He had to experience loneliness, rejection, betrayal, pain, suffering, and absolute desperation. In order to understand what it feels to be a flying bird, He had to experience solitude, determination, peace, confidence, hope, and success.

In order for Him to empathize with a bonded sinner, somehow Jesus had to experience that horror, too. There is no place you can go where Christ hasn't already been. There is nothing you can feel that He hasn't felt . . . be it sadness or celebration.

He worked, He sang, He studied, He laughed, He loved. He didn't give us five senses so that we would only use two and a half of them. No! Jesus tasted, touched, smelled, heard, and saw all life had to offer here in this land that His very presence made holy.

He didn't lag behind and wait to be prodded. He didn't waste an opportunity thinking it would pass His way again. Yet He always chose the better part, did not give in to the temptations of His flesh, did not yield. And when the devil came against Him in His most weakened state, the devil quoted scripture, and Jesus quoted scripture right back! "It is written," He said, because He'd studied, He'd memorized, He'd made the word part of who He was.

Jesus knew the pain of loss. His cousin John was beheaded by a madman. He knew the joy of return, for He raised His beloved brother Lazarus, and left his tomb empty, too.

He learned not only to give, but to receive. When the woman wanted to wash His feet with her tears and wipe them dry with her hair, when she wanted to pour her fragrance on Him, He didn't hold up His hand and say *No, don't do that . . . it's too much, it might give the wrong impression.*

Part of life is giving. Part is also receiving.

Jesus didn't just associate with His Apostles, His chosen. He cherished variety in people. Though we are created in the Father's image, we are all different. He picked His friends from every walk of life, from the wealthy to the poor, from the educated to the simple. I adore the story recorded in the nineteenth chapter of Luke: "And Jesus entered and passed through Jericho. And, behold, there was a man named Zacchaeus, which was the chief among the publicans, and he was rich. And he sought to see Jesus who he was; and could not for the press, because he was little of stature. And he ran before, and climbed up into a sycamore tree to see him: for he was to pass that way. And when Jesus came to the place, he looked up, and saw him, and said unto him, Zacchaeus, make haste, and come down; for to day I must abide at thy house. And he made haste, and came down, and received him joyfully."

What an example. Zacchaeus believed in Jesus. He deemed himself worthy, though others did not. He didn't let an obstacle stand in his way . . . he used it for a rise instead. He ran, he climbed, and he received joyfully!

What a lesson in that example.

Jesus sought to serve because He knew that was and always will be the best way to show forth love to the Father. Through service comes a reservoir of joy and healing. Back when I was so broken that it was impossible to lift my own head, the Spirit whispered to me, "Take your mind off your own troubles. I'll worry about them for you. You focus on my Son, and I'll focus on you . . . now go out and do some good for others."

It was through service that my own broken wings were bound up. It is through lack of service that they begin to weaken. President J. Reuben Clark taught this principle bluntly: "There is no greater blessing, no greater joy and happiness than comes to us from relieving the distress of others" ("Fundamentals of the Church Welfare Plan," *Church News,* Mar. 2, 1946, 9).

Jesus had to seek out the lepers because they were exiled and could not come to Him. He stopped for the beggars, went out among the people—the best way to immerse Himself in life. Yet, when the masses grew too maddening, when the pressures pressed too hard, Jesus got up and left. He went into the mountains, out on the sea, wherever He could find stillness and peace so He could communicate with the Father and have restored to Him all that He had given of Himself to others.

Then, when His time had come, everything that Jesus had become He laid at the altar as He walked willingly into a garden called Gethsemane.

There, among the olive trees and rocks and a few blades of growing grass, the greatest exchange that will ever occur took place. I don't pretend to understand how One whose value is beyond measure would be willing, even eager, to pay the price of MY sins, to take away my sorrows so that I too might know the joys of living life.

I love the Apostle Peter. Impetuous Peter, the only one who got out of the boat. The only one who took offense and sliced the ear of the high priest's servant. The emotions surrounding that incident both before and afterward are most telling. Read the 22nd chapter of Luke. I relate to Peter. At times I am too brash, too bold. I make mistakes with the best of intentions. I make mistakes without the best of intentions. I love my Savior, yet I've denied Him more than thrice with the words I say and don't say, with the acts I do and the acts I leave undone. Jesus healed the servant's ear, and I believe He forgave Peter then, knowing that what would happen in the coming hours would make it very difficult for Peter to forgive himself. Can't you just feel the love, the heart of Christ for Peter? For Jesus, it was all about forgiveness and giving another chance to the one who had tried to fly and had fallen. Already Jesus had extended a hand to a fallen, drowning Peter, and He would do it again and again until Peter finally understood that none of us is strong enough to make it on his or her own.

What a friend we have in Jesus!

What could I give in exchange for such a gift to me? I am just one flailing sparrow, and He is the Creator of Creation. The Father of countless sparrows.

Now . . . follow me to the end of my days in Jerusalem. I'm back at the temple, at the wall that Solomon had built. At the wall where tens of millions of prayers have been offered up.

I know the priest warned me that Christ's comfort cannot be found in a place, and yet I feel it here.

My eye catches the dive of a sparrow, soon joined by another, and another. I'm so full of gratitude I think my heart my will stop.

A mother teaching her young daughter how to approach the wall, how to read their holy words and pray in reverence, meets my smile. She asks in Hebrew if I will take a photograph of the two of them. I'm delighted, and I watch as they finish and step carefully away, backing up so that their backs are never turned to the sacred rise of the Western Wall.

I don't know how long I stay there basking in a spirit of life, of love and diversity, of hope in the midst of war.

"Turn," a voice whispers from within my soul. "Turn now."

I turn and I see it. A final tender mercy . . . for I find myself looking directly into the face of a baby boy. He is seated in a stroller while his mother prays. He is looking right at me, and I think that must be how Jesus looked when He was just a year old . . . eyes filled with light and love, a smile so powerful that the sun suddenly seems brighter. Ready to conquer the world. To live every moment to the fullest.

I start to back up, too, to show that I hold reverence for this sacred, sacred place, but I'm not sure of my step, and so I reach back to grasp the support of a white chair that is behind me. When I do, I feel a softness flutter over my hand, and I see a single sparrow circle so close to me I can hear its wings in flight.

It soars upward, circles once more, and takes refuge in a niche in the great wall. I realize that it's impossible for that bird to be the fallen sparrow outside my hotel window, but I imagine that it is. For with God, all things are possible. I lift my camera and I click, but it's not the photo taken by my camera that tells the story . . . it's the image taken in my heart.

Today I realize the infinite value of a single fallen sparrow. Today I know that the comfort of the Christ *is* found in a place. A place within our hearts. A place niched out for a God that not only gave us life, but demonstrated how to live it.

I vow that I will live more fully, more gratefully, more selflessly. I will celebrate a raindrop, and I will celebrate a rainbow.

My head bows, and with the sounds of weeping, wailing, praying, and fluttering wings around me, I say aloud, "Toda."

"Toda, Abba."